Prawle Point
and the Coast between
Start Point and Salcombe Bar

An Illustrated History

Roger Barret

G000059776

Published by the
National Coastwatch Institution, Prawle Point
Registered Charity No. 1045645

www. nci.org.uk
www.nci-prawlepoint.org.uk

Funded by the Heritage Lottery Fund
as part of the NCI Prawle Point Visitor Centre Project

*All profits from the sale of this book will be used
to maintain the watch at the NCI Prawle Point Lookout.*

Printed by
Kingfisher Print and Design Ltd, Totnes, Devon

Dedication and Acknowledgements

This book is dedicated to the volunteers in the following local organisations that help to protect the lives of those that venture along the coast:

HM Prawle Point Coastguard Rescue Team
RNLI Lifeboat, Salcombe
NCI Prawle Point

My sincere thanks to all those who helped in some way with the completion of this book, particularly Richard and Jane Partridge of East Prawle who kindly provided me with much valuable material. Other well-informed local residents who assisted include Jonathan Ansell, Jeanne James, Bill Login, and farmers Roger Tucker and Derek Wotton. Also of great help were Jim Tyson of the South West Maritime Archaeological Group; Dr. Ben Roberts, Curator of the European Bronze Age at the British Museum; and staff at the Cookworthy Museum, Kingsbridge. My thanks also to Jenny Brown and Theresa Thomson for checking the typescript, to my National Coastwatch colleagues for their support and to the Heritage Lottery Fund for funding the project.

The help given by all those who supplied illustrations is also gratefully acknowledged. Every effort has been made to trace copyright holders and the author and publisher apologise if any have been inadvertently omitted.

Published by the National Coastwatch Institution, Prawle Point
PO Box 58, Kingsbridge, Devon, TQ7 2ZQ

ISBN 978 0 9568854 0 1

Also by Roger Barrett:
Start Point and Its Lighthouse: History, Map and Guide

Contents

Maps

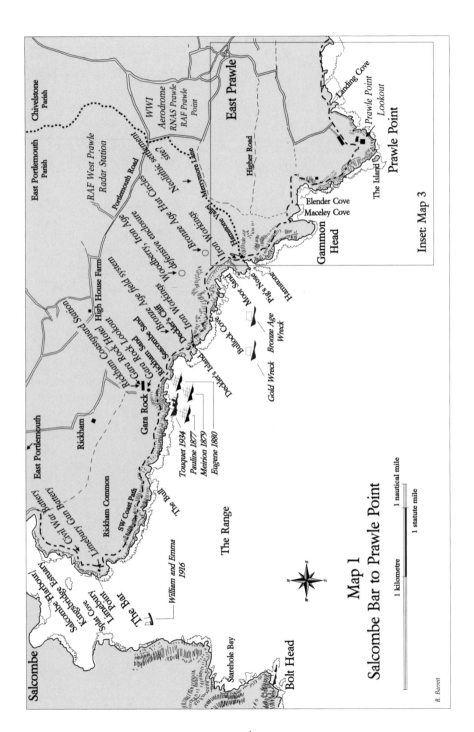

Salcombe

Kingsbridge Estuary
Salcombe Harbour

East Portlemouth

Rickham

Rickham Common

SW Coast Path

The Bull

Spat Cove
Limebury Point
The Bar

Limebury Gun Battery
Civil War Gun Battery

William and Emma
1916

Chivelstone
Parish

East Portlemouth
Parish

WWI
Aerodrome
RNAS Prawle
RAF Prawle
Point

RAF West Prawle
Radar Station

Portlemouth Road

Neolithic settlement

Merrymore Lane

Bronze Age Hut Circles

Woodbury, Iron Age
defensive enclosure

Iron Workings

Iron Workings

Decker's Cliff
Bronze Age

Seacombe Sand

Rickham Sand

Gara Rock

High House Farm

Rickham Coastguard Station
Gara Rock Hotel
Gara Rock Lookout

Touquet 1934
Pauline 1877
Metrion 1879
Eugene 1880

Decker's Island

Moor Sand

Bullock Cove

Gold Wreck

Bronze Age
Wreck

Pig's Nose

Hanstone

Gammon
Head

East Prawle

Higher Road

Higher Road

Hanstone Valley

Elender Cove
Maceley Cove

Landing Cove

Prawle Point
Lookout

The Island

Prawle Point

Inset: Map 3

The Range

StareHole Bay

Bolt Head

Map 1
Salcombe Bar to Prawle Point

1 kilometre

1 nautical mile

1 statute mile

R. Barrett

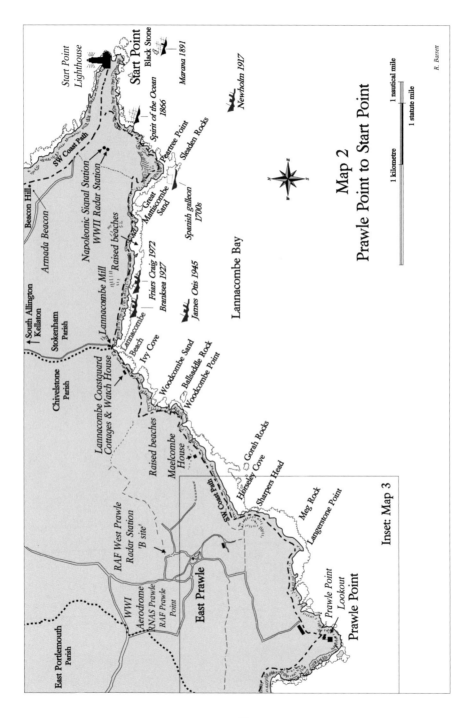

Map 2
Prawle Point to Start Point

Inset: Map 3

R. Barrett

v

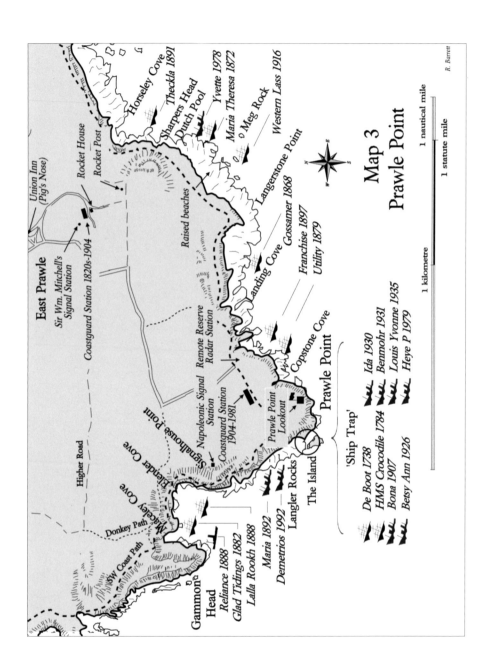

Map 3
Prawle Point

Union Inn
(Pig's Nose)

East Prawle

Sir Wm. Mitchell's
Signal Station

Rocket House

Rocket Post

Coastguard Station 1820s-1904

Horseley Cove

Thekla 1891

Sharpers Head
Dutch Pool

Yvette 1978

Maria Theresa 1872

Meg Rock

Western Lass 1916

Langerstone Point

Raised beaches

Landing Cove
Gossamer 1868

Franchise 1897

Utility 1879

Higher Road

Napoleonic Signal
Station

Remote Reserve
Radar Station

Coastguard Station
1904-1981

Signalhouse Point

Copstone Cove

Prawle Point
Lookout

Prawle Point

Elender Cove

Maceley Cove

Donkey Path

SW Coast Path

Gammon
Head

Reliance 1888

Glad Tidings 1882

Lalla Rookh 1888

Maria 1892

Demetrios 1992

Langler Rocks

The Island

'Ship Trap'

De Boot 1738

HMS Crocodile 1784

Bona 1907

Betsy Ann 1926

Ida 1930

Benmohr 1931

Louis Yvonne 1935

Heye P 1979

1 kilometre

1 nautical mile

1 statute mile

R. Barrett

vi

1. INTRODUCTION

The southernmost point in Devon. A view of Prawle Point from the east, with the National Coastwatch Lookout on top of the headland and Arch Rock , the 'Horse's Head', at its foot

Guarding the Coast

Between Start Point to the east and Salcombe Bar – at the mouth of the Salcombe-Kingsbridge Estuary – to the west, can be found some of the finest coastal scenery in Devon. Reached only by winding lanes and still unspoilt, this eight mile stretch of coast is now protected for its beauty, wildlife and impressive geology as a Site of Special Scientific Interest and as part of an Area of Outstanding Natural Beauty. At its centre, the rugged promontory of Prawle Point, the southernmost tip of Devon, rises nearly 200 feet (60 metres) above the sea. Once famous as a Lloyd's Signal Station, the old coastguard lookout standing sentinel on its top is today manned by the volunteers of the National Coastwatch Institution who keep a sharp lookout for the safety of those who venture along the coast.

Well-known to mariners past and present, Prawle Point and the long jagged peninsula of Start Point three miles to the east, have always been important landfalls and waymarks for ships and their crews plying the busy trade routes of the English Channel. Sadly for many, the rockbound shores of these great headlands have also been their graveyard.

In Old English, Prawle Point means *Lookout Hill* and throughout the centuries people have gathered here to look out, not only 'for those in peril on the sea' but also, during unsettled times, for invaders, raiders, pirates or smugglers. The waters around this exposed and inhospitable coast have

1

always been a source of danger and the few buildings that have been erected along its shores were built for those charged with its protection. In the last three hundred years these have included three coastguard stations, four lookout posts, a lighthouse, four signal stations, several gun batteries and two Second World War radar stations. During the same period as few as five buildings are known to have been erected purely for civilian use.

In spite of the sparseness of its population and its remoteness, this is a coast that is steeped in history and many great and stirring events have been witnessed by those who have kept vigil here. The threats from the sea have come in many forms, from Danish longboats, the ships and galleys of the Spanish Armada, pirates and privateers, smuggling craft, mariners at risk in storm and fog, and, in the last century, German U-boats, E-boats and fighter aircraft. However, the duties of those tasked with watching and guarding this coast have varied little: to provide early warning of hostile forces, to prevent and stamp out illegal activities such as smuggling, to protect and support legitimate trade or to safeguard life at sea.

Over the centuries, all of these roles have been carried out, in varying degrees, along this now peaceful stretch of coastline, by uniformed coast-guards, military defenders and coast watchers. Indeed it could be said that the history of Prawle Point and the surrounding coast is the history of the defence and protection of our island shores in microcosm.

The Character of the Coast

Backed by impressive cliffs, this is a coastline of rugged headlands,

hidden coves and caves, and treacherous offshore rocks. To the east is the long and exposed headland of Start Point with its iconic lighthouse. The narrow spine of Start Point is capped by jagged outcrops of mica schist rock, first formed as sediments on the sea bed in the Devonian Period nearly 400 million years ago and then metamorphosed during a mountain building phase in the subsequent Carboniferous Period.

Start Point and its lighthouse viewed from Peartree Point

The craggy slopes at Start sweep round to the prominent headland of Peartree Point, beyond which the coastline takes on a different character.

From Peartree to Prawle Point, five miles to the west, an irregular terrace of low-lying fields is backed by a broken line of weathered cliffs formed at a time of higher sea levels.

Great Mattiscombe Sand looking west to Prawle Point

During the last Ice Age the bedrock above these cliffs was shattered by frost action and rocky particles known as 'head' slid down the cliffs to form a gently sloping terrace of varying width. To seaward the rocky shelves above the shoreline are fine examples of wave cut platforms and raised beaches formed in warmer inter-glacial periods when sea levels were higher than today.

View from Woodcombe Point to Sharper's Head showing the terrace of small fields

Other features along this coast are the jutting headlands at Woodcombe Point and Sharper's Head and, between the raised beaches, the shingle beach at Horseley Cove and the attractive sandy coves of Great Mattiscombe Sand and Lannacombe Beach. Treacherous reefs lie just offshore at Ballsaddle Rock, Gorah Rocks and the Meg.

The raised beaches east of Prawle Point

Rounding the low lying Langerstone Point, the shiny mica schist rocks give way to rocks of a greener hue – hornblende schists of a similar age to the mica schists.

At Prawle Point these rocks – weatherbeaten by the prevailing south-westerlies and the long Atlantic swells – have been greatly eroded and, at the base of the headland, wind and waves have created an impressive natural archway shaped like a horse's head. To the west, separating Prawle Point from a rocky outlier known simply as the Island, is a narrow 'gut' or channel which has gained an evil reputation over the years as a graveyard of ships: the Prawle Point 'Ship Trap'.

The western side of Prawle Point below the Lookout. The narrow channel between the Point and the Island is known as the Prawle Point 'Ship Trap'

To the west the coastal slopes between Prawle Point and Limebury Point are hemmed in by the high plateau above and the rocky shelves below and so tend to be more precipitous than those to the east. Gammon Head is particularly dramatic, its rocky spur towering above the secluded Maceley and Elender Coves.

Gammon Head with Maceley Cove below and Elender Cove to the right

Here the coastal features take on something of a 'porcine quality', for just to the west of Gammon Head are to be found the Pig's Nose and the Ham

Looking west from the Ham Stone and the Pig's Nose to Limebury Point

4

Stone, whilst further to the west they become distinctly 'bovine' with Bullock Cove and the Bull. Another dominant feature is Gara Rock rising above Rickham and Seacombe Sands and capped by its distinctive thatched lookout. Rocky gorse and bracken-covered slopes extend as far as Limebury Point at the mouth of the Salcombe-Kingsbridge Estuary. Dominating the view on the far side of the estuary are the high cliffs of Bolt Head and Sharp Tor. Rising seas at the end of the last Ice Age cut through the resistant schist rocks between Limebury Point and Bolt Head flooding the inland valleys to form the magnificent ria or flooded estuary.

Extending across the mouth of the estuary is Salcombe Bar – a large spit of sand with a least depth of 0.7 metres at low tide. Dangerous to navigate on a falling tide and with the wind in the south or south east, the Bar has claimed many lives over the years.

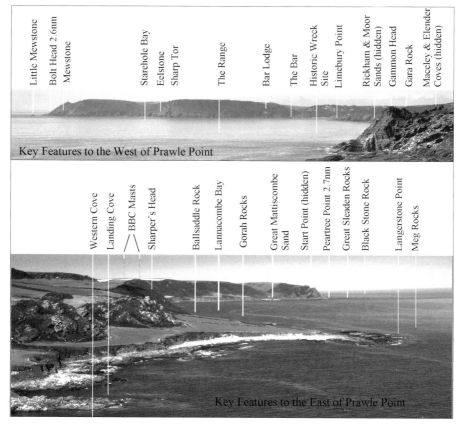

Key Features to the West of Prawle Point

Key Features to the East of Prawle Point

2. EARLY HISTORY

Prehistory

Flint tools found along this coast suggest that it was occupied by hunter gatherers at the end of the last Ice Age, at a time when sea levels were several metres lower than today. Tools and scatters of flint waste, believed to be from the Mesolithic period (14,000 to 6,500 years ago), have been found between Lannacombe and Start Point, on Woodcombe Sand, and also near Langerstone Point and on the cliff path west of Gara Rock.

The Hamstone valley above Moor Sand – a possible area of Neolithic and Bronze Age settlement

The Neolithic period (6,500 to 4,500 years ago) saw the first settled farming communities. Robert Waterhouse, in his East Portlemouth Heritage Appraisal, considers that one possible settlement site was in the Hamstone valley, east of Moor Sand. Dense scatters of flintmaking debris have been found here 'on a south facing slope near several springs of water. This would have been the ideal place to live – far enough inland to be sheltered from storms, with the sea only a short walk away for fishing and shellfish collection'. A polished greenstone axe and a flint arrowhead have also been found nearby.

Definite evidence of settled farming communities dates to the Bronze and Iron Ages (4,500 to 2,000 years ago). Ancient field systems, with distinctive parallel field banks, can be seen just to the north of Prawle Point – where the field boundaries are marked by rows of large flat stone slabs set on edge – and at Deckler's Cliff near Gara Rock. The 'co-axial' field system at Deckler's Cliff covers about four hectares and survives as a complex group of field banks on the south side of a valley. On its southern edge two small groups of circular stone huts have been identified. A little to the east, aerial photography has revealed a small settlement, possibly a village of Bronze Age date, with at least five circular stone walled huts, on the slopes above Moor Sand. Further inland Bronze Age burial mounds (round barrows) were sited on hilltops and, in Chivelstone Parish, a find of two rare polished greenstone mace heads, used for ceremonial purposes, may represent the grave goods of a high-ranking individual.

It is possible that this was a community of traders as well as farmers for, on the seabed just west of Gammon Head, are two, possibly three Bronze Age shipwrecks. Dating back over 3,000 years, and amongst the oldest shipwrecks in the world, they provide evidence of strong trading links with Europe during the Bronze Age.

The Deckler's Cliff Bronze and Iron Age field systems to the east of Gara Rock

The first finds were made in 1976 when diver Phil Baker discovered a fine bronze sword on what is now the protected Moor Sand Site. Later finds on this site included six swords or sword fragments, and two bronze axes (palstaves) dating to 1300-800BC.

Between 2002 and 2008 divers from the South West Maritime Archaeological Group (SWMAG) found a total of 53 Bronze Age artefacts, dating to the 1300-1150BC period, on the nearby Salcombe Cannon site (the seventeenth century AD Gold Wreck site described on page 11). They included palstaves, rapier blades, gold torcs and two exceptionally rare and intricate gold wire bracelets. One of the bronze objects, a *strumento*, is found only in Sicily, suggesting close links with the Mediterranean.

A further major discovery was made by the SWMAG diving team in 2009. This second, or even third, shipwreck site, dating to 1300-800BC, was apparently that of a vessel carrying a valuable cargo of tin and copper either to or from the Continent. The finds include 259 copper and 27 tin ingots,

Gold braided jewellery and Bronze Axes or Palstaves c1300-1150BC from the Bronze Age Wreck Sites. (Left: SWMAG. Right: Trustees of the British Museum))

7

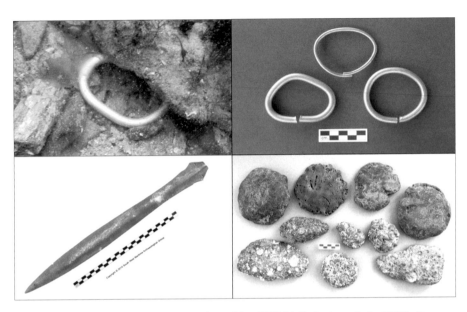

Artefacts dating to 1000-900BC found by SWMAG during their 2009 dive off Moor Sand. Top: Gold wrist torcs. Bottom left: Leaf Sword Bottom right: Copper and tin ingots - used for making bronze (SWMAG)

a bronze leaf sword and three gold bar bracelets. The copper ingots form the largest single collection of their kind in Britain, whilst the tin ingots are the first, belonging to the Bronze Age period, to have been recovered west of Turkey. These exciting discoveries provide clear evidence of a sophisticated trade in bulk goods with continental Europe during the Bronze Age.

From about 1000BC, climate change forced the people of the late Bronze Age to abandon their settlements on Dartmoor. This gave rise to population pressure along the coast, and defended sites and bronze weaponry provide evidence of territorial conflict during the late Bronze Age and into the Iron Age. An oval enclosure to the east of the Deckler's Cliff field system known as Woodberry may have provided some protection for the farming community and their stock. Slight remains of entrenchments at nearby Prawle Point, suggesting a possible promontory fort, were identified in the 1906 edition of the Victorian County History of Devon. Perhaps Prawle Point served as a defensive site for the Bronze and Iron Age settlers, albeit on a much smaller scale than the impressive promontory fort at Bolt Tail to the west.

The Early Christian Period

Fifteen hundred years on, Prawle Point may well have taken on a special significance for the early Christians. A reference in Adam of Bremen's *Historia Ecclesiastica*, written about 1080, suggests that Prawle was a station or port on the voyages made by Christian pilgrims from Denmark to the Holy Land. Other stations on the route, including the shrine of St. Matthew in Brittany and La Corunna for Santiago de Compestella in Spain, had an obvious significance for Christian pilgrims. So what attracted them across the Channel to Prawle?

St. Brendan the Navigator

Perhaps there was a connection with St. Brendan the Navigator (c484-c577)? A chapel dedicated to St. Brendan, is known to have existed at Prawle in 1420. During the Middle Ages small chapels were built along the coast on headlands to provide a guiding light for mariners. St. Michael's Chapel at Rame Head is a surviving example, whilst at Start Point there is a reference to the Blessed Mary of Start. W.G. Hoskins, the eminent historian, writing in 1954, stated that 'St. Brendan the Navigator rounded the foaming Start and raised a chapel on the headland of Prawle'. Percy Russell in 1955, considered that the natural site of the chapel at Prawle would be on 'the great rock at Prawle Point which bears the Lloyd's signal station' (now the National Coastwatch Lookout). However, local historian Jeanne James has studied the available evidence in detail and believes that the chapel was sited in Chapel Field, East Prawle.

Surviving records, such as the Domesday survey, tell us little about this coast during the medieval period, not least because exposure to storms and hostile raiders discouraged settlement. Much of the coastal fringe was barren heathland, with human activity largely confined to seasonal fishing, the collection of sand and seaweed to fertilise inland fields, and 'beachcombing' for flotsam and jetsam cast up on the shore.

Prawle Point – the Saxon 'Lookout Hill' – and Beacon Hill above Start Point to the east, would almost certainly have been used as vantage points in times of danger. From promontories such as these, the Saxons mounted a system of 'watch and ward' and relied on messengers to spread the warning rather than using fire. The first mention of fire beacons in public records was in 1326 and throughout the Hundred Years War (1337-1453) orders were sent out for beacon fires to be prepared along the Channel coast.

The Spanish Armada 1588

During the Elizabethan period, local militia were raised and trained to defend the coast against invasion from Catholic Spain. The surviving Muster Rolls for 1569 tell us that, in East Portlemouth and Chivelstone parishes, twelve of the better-off citizens were required to pay for equipment whilst 61 able-bodied men (18 from Portlemouth and 43 from Chivelstone, which includes East Prawle) were called upon to serve as archers, harquebusiers (armed with an early form of musket), pikemen and billmen.

The Court Rolls of Stokenham Manor and the Stokenham Parish Register provide an occasional insight into local life at this time – in 1576 Roger Partridge was fined for blocking the path at Horseley Sand and in 1582 a ship called the *Emanuel* came ashore there, laden with fish and all of its equipment and, rather surprisingly, was still there a fortnight later. On 1 November 1587 a 'bombard' gun carriage came ashore at 'Prall' as wreckage. More dramatically there are references, in 1581, to pirates. An entry in the Parish Register records that 'a pirate of the sea was hanged in chains upon Stert (Start Point) on the 28th day of September, in the year of our Lord 1581. His name was Henry Muge'. In July and October of that year the Stokenham Court Rolls refer to items taken from pirates: three swords, a dagger, a sharp rapier, money and a silver 'tothepecker and earepeker'.

In 1586 a chain of beacons was set up to warn of invasion and when King Philip of Spain's Great Armada of 1588 was first sighted off the Lizard in Cornwall, at dawn on 30 July, the fire beacons immediately flashed their warning along the coast. In the South Hams the beacon light passed in a chain through Thurlestone, Malborough, South Pool, Chivelstone, to the watchmen at Beacon Hill, above Start Bay. Their flames were then passed to Dartmouth, and on to London.

Whether or not Prawle Point played its part as a beacon site is not known but in the fading light of Sunday evening, 31 July 1588, local people would have gathered there, as

An engraving with the rather fanciful title 'The Defeat of the Spanish Armada off the Start Point near Plymouth'

well as above Start Point, to witness a spectacle of unsurpassed magnitude as 'the greatest navy that ever swam the sea' sailed by in slow procession. Spread over seven miles of water, in crescent formation, were 125 Spanish ships. Two miles astern, the English fleet – 105 vessels commanded by Lord Howard of Effingham – passed by as darkness fell. The Great Armada sailed on towards Portland Bill but, with much of it later driven onshore by English fireships and a 'Protestant wind', only a shattered remnant would return to Spain.

Pirate Gold

In 1995, a group of divers belonging to the South West Maritime Archaeological Group, literally struck gold when they found four coins on the seabed between Gara Rock and Moor Sands. They had been searching the area following an earlier find of four cannon. (The protected site is known as the Salcombe Cannon site.) Over the next two years a treasure trove of 447 gold coins, as well as gold jewellery and ingots, pewter and pottery, were brought to the surface.

The coins were struck by the Sa'dian dynasty who ruled in Morocco for one hundred years from the mid-sixteenth century. The last coins found helped to date the wreck. They belonged to a ruler called Sharif al-Walid who ruled between 1631 and 1636. The pieces of gold jewellery – earrings, brooches and bracelets – were all cut in half and are believed to be a cargo of scrap pieces for melting down into finger ingots.

Another theory is that the broken pieces represent a division of pirates' loot, with one half for the captain and crew, the other for the ship owners and financial backers. In addition to the North African treasure, the finds included a number of artefacts of Dutch origin, including pewter table-ware, stoneware wine decanters, Delft pottery, and an ornate clay pipe

Coins and Jewellery from the Gold Wreck site (SWMAG)

Jewellery items and a gold finger ingot from the Gold Wreck site,
also known as the Salcombe Cannon Site (SWMAG)

made in the Netherlands between 1635 and 1645. The finds, now in the British Museum, represent one of the most important collections of gold ever found in European waters.

The evidence points to a wreck of around 1640 and one theory is that the vessel was a Dutch merchantman returning from the Mediterranean. However, many experts believe that she was a Barbary Pirate ship sunk whilst raiding the South Devon coast for white slaves to take back to North Africa. In the early 1600s Barbary Pirates terrorised the coasts of Devon and Cornwall making them so 'dangerous through their spoils as few dared put forth of their harbours'. If the pirate theory is correct then the name of the nearby beach, Moor Sand, may well have its origins in this event.

English Civil War 1642-6

Although this coastal area was largely untouched by the ravages of the English Civil War, nearby Salcombe was a favourite base for Royalist priva-teers and a number of contemporary references tell of Royalist ships being chased into Salcombe by the Parliamentary navy and by Dunkirk privateers. In January 1646 Parliamentary troops came in force to the area, marching along the Portlemouth road to lay siege to Fort Charles on the opposite side of Salcombe Harbour. Bringing up heavy guns from Dartmouth they established a battery on Rickham Common and bombarded the fort until it capitulated on 9 May 1646. It was one of the last Royalist strongholds in the West to fall.

Fort Charles guarding Salcombe Harbour. Water colour by Rev. J. Swete 1794

3. WRECKS, WRECKERS AND SMUGGLERS

The Wreck of *De Boot* 1738

The earliest recorded wreck on Prawle Point was on 20 October 1738 and involved the 650 ton Dutch East Indiaman *De Boot*. On a return voyage from the Dutch East Indies laden with tea, Chinese porcelain and uncut diamonds and rubies, *De Boot* encountered severe weather as she made her way up-channel, and was blown onto the Island, just off Prawle Point. Two of the crew were washed overboard. Realising his ship was lost, the captain attempted to save the boxes of precious stones by passing them along a chain of men to the shore. As the waves grew in size, a local man jumped from the rocks into the surging water, and the captain, struggling with the last box, passed it to him. 'The fellow' reached the shore and then 'had the modesty to march off with the same, and has not been since heard of!'

HMS Crocodile 1784

HMS Crocodile was a 24 gun, sixth rate frigate built in Portsmouth in 1781. Returning with despatches from India with a crew of 170 men, she ran into thick fog off Prawle Point in the early hours of 9 May 1784 and went aground in the narrow channel between the Island and the west side of Prawle Point. Captain Williamson ordered his men to cut away the masts and throw guns and tackle overboard to lighten her. It was to no avail and so, with the water rising fast, he collected his precious despatches and gave the order to abandon ship.

Williamson requisitioned a barn in East Prawle as sleeping quarters, but the men proved difficult to control. The Master, calling one man, William Smith, to his duty, was dealt a violent blow for his pains, which left him unconscious. Smith, a bosun's mate, realising that he had committed a capital offence, took to his heels and was not seen again.

On the second day ashore, a seaman, Patrick Crawley, already the worse for drink, entered the house where a master's mate and a petty officer were lodging and demanded 'grog'. In the scuffle that followed Crawley struck the petty officer, an offence for which Crawley was subsequently sentenced to be flogged round the fleet at Portsmouth with 100 lashes.

Back at Prawle the work of salvaging the *Crocodile's* guns, anchors, cables, sails and stores went on, but with the ship on its beam ends and with gales and heavy seas, it was no easy task. Eventually, however, the anchors and nearly all the guns were recovered and shipped off to Plymouth.

At his court martial, Captain Williamson was criticised for his failure to use the sounding lead when he knew his ship was in restricted waters in fog. Over two hundred years later, diver Terry Crocker acquired the wreck from the Ministry of Defence. His finds included a cannon, cannonballs, musket balls as well as Williamson's 'neglected' sounding lead.

Wreckers

Whilst it is unlikely that ships were deliberately lured by guiding lights onto the rocks along this coast by wreckers, the looting of shipwrecks was common practice. Between 1236 and 1771 the law sanctioned the pillage of wrecks provided no man or beast survived. It was a law that invited murder.

During the 1700s the parson at East Portlemouth was interrupted in his sermon with news of a wreck, whereupon he informed his assembled flock that 'there's a ship ashore between Prawle and Peartree Point. One more prayer, and we'll all start fair'. Rushing to Great Mattiscombe Sand, the parson and his congregation found a valuable Spanish ship on the rocks. Local legend has it that the stranded crew shouted for a rope, but the one that was thrown was too short, and when the cry went up for 'more rope!', the hapless mariners were abandoned to their fate because 'dead men told no tales'.

Perhaps it was the bones of one of these dead men that were found exposed in an eroded cliff near Peartree Point in the 1970s. Until 1808 the bodies of shipwreck victims were generally buried close to where they were cast ashore but, from that date, the Burial of Drowned Persons Act required that their graves should be in consecrated ground. More human bones were exca-vated in 2003, at Landing Cove to the west. Radio-carbon dating of these suggested a man aged over 29 who drowned in the late 18th or early 19th century.

Wreckage

When the manorial courts held sway, up until the sev-enteenth century, the lords of Stokenham Manor rigorously enforced the devolved royal right to seize unclaimed items of

Great Mattiscombe or 'Matchcombe' Sand. Also known, according to local legend, as 'More Rope Bay' following a wrecking incident

wreckage cast up on the shore. The surviving Elizabethan Court Rolls of Stokenham Manor contain numerous references to small boats, parts of ships and their rigging as well as items of their cargo (such as hogsheads of wine and bales of Spanish wool) washed up along the coast near 'Prall' and 'Lanacombe'. Finds were presented at the manor court and those materials unclaimed for a year and a day were sold for the lord's benefit, although it was the custom of the manor that one half of the proceeds went to the finder.

Smugglers

Towards the end of the eighteenth century smuggling was being carried out on a large scale by the residents of East Prawle or, as they were styled by one informer, 'those Prawl People'. In 1783 Richard Valentine, the Customs officer at Salcombe, reported that the local people along this coast, 'who are in general poor', were actively engaged in bringing the goods ashore from the smuggling vessels. 'The species of ship employed on this coast are chiefly fishing craft belonging to Torbay who generally land their cargoes on or near the Start or Prawle. At these places myself and the rest of the officers under my direction have kept a constant look-out at nights when the wind is fair, and in times past have made considerable seizures, but the smugglers have altered their proceedings which is that they never land any goods before the horses are in readiness on the spot to take the same away, which are seldom less in number than fifty and oftentimes a hundred at a time. Every horse has his rider armed with a loaded whip or a brace of pistols in order to despatch the officers if they attempt to make seizure of the goods...' Richard Valentine had himself been threatened with having his brains blown out, but he nevertheless considered that he

Waiting to guide the smugglers' boat ashore (Fred Roe)

could deal with the problem, given more help: 'if there was about twelve or fourteen of the horse troop stationed at Kingsbridge, they'd give a good account of themselves'.

So where did the self-styled 'free traders' bring their contraband ashore? The secluded beach at Lannacombe was an obvious possibility, offering a safe approach and good access to the inland villages of South Allington and

Kellaton. Further west the coast at Horseley Cove is rather flat and open but, with easy access up to East Prawle, may have been used before the Preventive Station was built on the hill above in the early 1800s.

To the west of Prawle Point, the coves below Gammon Head – Maceley and Elender Coves –

Lannacombe Beach

Maceley and Elender Coves with Gammon Head beyond

certainly have the 'feel' of a smuggler's haunt. Above the cliffs, old pathways lead inland. One, the Donkey Path, connects with two old green lanes, Merrymore Lane and Higher Road, both of which lead to East Prawle where the Pig's Nose Inn, formerly the Union Inn, is alleged to have been a place of storage and disposal.

Finally, the two beaches below Gara Rock, Rickham and Seacombe Sands, would have provided a safe landing and good access via inland tracks to East Portlemouth where the tower of St. Winwaloe's Church was reputedly used for the storage of contraband, no doubt with the inducement of some 'brandy for the Parson and baccy for the Clerk'.

Seacombe and Rickham Sands

16

4. FIGHTING THE FRENCH 1793-1815

The 'Battle of Prawle Point' 1793

The first naval action in home waters, on the outbreak of war against Revolutionary France in 1793, took place off Prawle Point. The sea fight was between *HMS Nymphe* and the French National Frigate *Cleopatre*. According to the Naval Chronicle, 'the capture of the *Cleopatre*, 40 guns, 320 men, by Captain Edward Pellew, in the *Nymphe*, 36 guns, 250 men, on the 18th of June, was accomplished with a gallantry not to be paralleled in any country but our own, and vindicated the superiority of the British navy'.

Sir Edward Pellew, later Viscount Exmouth

Equally jingoistic in its tone is this stirring account of the action recounted by Ellen Luscombe of Salcombe in 1861:

'Mr. Edwards saw this battle from Prawle Point; and doubtless, as his eye kindled, and his blood swept through his veins in quickened rout, he longed, as any Englishman would long, to be in the midst of the fury of the fray. He saw the *Nymphe,* commanded by Pellew beating up channel, on the morning of 18 June 1793, a few miles to the south-west of the Start. At 6am she fell in with a French ship of war, the *Cleopatre*. A furious cannonade followed, which was kept up until seven o'clock by both vessels, when the *Nymphe* was skilfully laid alongside of her opponent; and in ten minutes every Frenchman was driven from the decks of the *Cleopatre* by the irresistible rush of the sailors of Pellew, who had thus gallantly won the first-fruits of the long series of naval engagements which immediately followed'.

HMS Nymphe (right) engaging the French National ship Cleopatre

Fighting their way aft, the British sailors reached the *Cleopatre*'s quarterdeck and

17

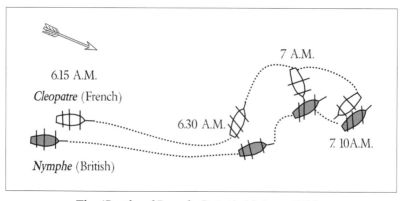

The 'Battle of Prawle Point', 18 June 1793

hauled down her colours. The French captain, Captain Mullon, who was lying mortally wounded on the deck, pulled a paper from his pocket, tore it to pieces and, whilst attempting to swallow it, died. The poor man had believed he was destroying the secret French signals, but in fact he had eaten his own commission, and so the signals fell into British hands.

Pellew put a prize crew aboard the *Cleopatre*, and *Nymphe* headed down wind to Portsmouth with the battered *Cleopatre* in her wake. When Pellew arrived on 21 June it was to a hero's welcome. Rewarded with a knighthood, he did not forget the widow of his gallant opponent, sending her her husband's belongings and a sum of money to 'ease her grief'.

Admiralty Signal Stations

When war with France broke out in 1793, the Channel coast was exposed to the threat of commerce raiding and invasion. To counter this, the Admiralty set up a series of 'early warning' signal stations in prominent coastal locations. 'Each station was commanded by a half-pay Naval Lieutenant, assisted by a Petty Officer or Midshipman and two men, all men considered unsuitable for ship service, probably by reason of their age.' They lived on site in a two-roomed hut. The 1795 signal station at Prawle was located above the present Lookout on what was then known as Hurter's Top, but is now called Signalhouse Point. Still to be seen is the stone base of a rectangular building sited to allow a clear line of sight to, and from, the flanking stations at West Soar to the west and on the 394 feet (120m) hill above Start Point to the east.

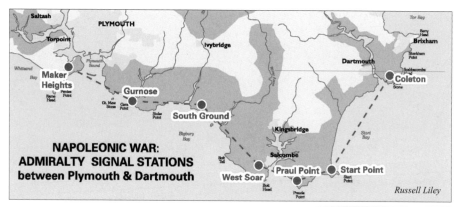

NAPOLEONIC WAR:
ADMIRALTY SIGNAL STATIONS
between Plymouth & Dartmouth

Russell Liley

Right: The remains of the Admiralty Signal Station above Prawle Point.

The station had a clear line of sight to the stations at West Soar four miles to the west and Start Point three miles to the east

West Soar Signal Station

Coded messages were sent by various combinations of pennant, flag, or ball. For example, the flag flying on the mast while three balls hung from the gaff signified 'enemy landing to the westward'. For night signals furze faggots or tar barrels were burnt in a beacon. Suspicious coastal shipping was then investigated by fast naval sloops, after warnings had been passed along the chain to Maker Heights above Plymouth.

A typical Napoleonic War Admiralty Signal Station. A naval lieutenant, a midshipman and two seamen lived in the two-room signal house (John Goodwin)

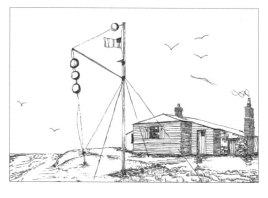

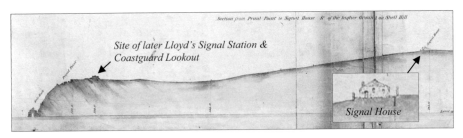

Site of later Lloyd's Signal Station &
Coastguard Lookout

Signal House

A sectional drawing of Prawle Point by James Walker, the engineer of Start Point Lighthouse, dated 1834. The inset shows the Signal House above Prawle Point (Trinity House)

'Old Boney' off Prawle Point 1815

The sea off Prawle Point was the scene not only of the first naval episode in home waters in the 1793-1815 wars with France – which commenced with the Battle of Prawle Point in 1793 – but also the last. On 18 June 1815, the Emperor Napoleon Bonaparte, after his defeat at Waterloo, surrendered to Captain Maitland of *HMS Bellerophon* (affectionately known as the *'Billy Ruffian'*) at Rochefort. Maitland sailed with his prisoner first to Brixham and then to Plymouth. Besieged by sightseers in both ports, the *Bellerophon* was ordered to cruise off Start Point with the 80-gun ship *Tonnant* and escorting frigates and await the arrival of *HMS Northumberland,* which was to transport Bonaparte to exile on St. Helena.

For two days the ships waited off the coast between Start Point, to the east of Prawle, and Bolt Head to the west. 'The grey sea under the louring, grey sky seemed to reflect the air of gloom which had settled over the passengers on the *Bellerophon*. Napoleon became increasingly depressed. He no longer appeared on deck but remained shut in his cabin … at one stage he talked about ending his life' *(David Cordingly).*

On 8 August Napoleon and his followers transferred to *HMS Northumberland* and then 'vanished into exile over the horizon'.

Napoleon on board the Bellerophon. Oil painting by Sir William Quiller (Tate Gallery, London)

5. THE PREVENTIVE SERVICE AT EAST PRAWLE AND RICKHAM

East Prawle Coastguard Station 1822 to 1856

After the fall of Napoleon in 1815, the south coast signal stations continued in operation, communicating with revenue vessels as well as with ships of the Royal Navy. Smuggling was still being carried on along the coast between Prawle and Start as a Preventive Station was built near East Prawle after the Preventive Water Guard was formed in 1809. Launching their boat from Horseley Cove, the men of the Water Guard would have rowed guard in Lannacombe Bay by night, or patrolled the coast on shore when it was too rough or foggy to launch.

In 1822 all of the forces concerned with the prevention of smuggling – the preventive water guard, revenue cruisers, and riding officers – were consolidated into a single force, under the direction of the Board of Customs, and from that date were officially known as the Coast Guard (later contracted to 'Coastguard'), but still referred to as the Preventive service.

The Prawle Coastguard Station (1823-1904) at Seaview Cottages or Newhouses, East Prawle

The terrace of six old coastguard cottages at Seaview, which formed the East Prawle Coastguard Station, was built about this time (the Board of Customs' lease commenced on 1 January 1823).

Apart from the chief officer's house at the western end, the cottages were just 'two up, two down' and so the living space was cramped. Coastguard families, like Victorian families generally, were large by today's standards. Chief Boatman, Nicholas Evans, who was buried in Chivelstone churchyard in 1843 after falling to his death at Landing Cove, left a wife and seven children to mourn his loss. Richard Merrifield, a boatman from Cornwall, also had seven children when he lived in one of the cottages in 1851.

Sanitation was basic with just a communal pit at the rear. At a later stage each cottage had its outside 'necessary'. The communal wash-house was at the eastern end, near the well. A degree of self-sufficiency was always encouraged to minimise reliance on the local population, and so pigs were kept in the steeply sloping back gardens. Fraternisation with the locals was also discouraged by the high iron railings and locked gates that once surrounded the buildings.

Extract from the 1827 Greenwood Map showing the Signal Post at Prawle Point and the Preventive Station below East Prawle

The site of the Preventive Station is marked on the 1827 Greenwood Map. It appears to be nearer to the coast than the old Coastguard Cottages at Seaview and it is likely that the station watchhouse was originally located above Sharper's Head, where the ivy-covered remains of a stone lookout still stand today. (In 1892 a half-acre plot of land here, known as the Stroll, was occupied by the Admiralty on a 1,000 year lease created in 1832.)

Until the Rickham station was opened in 1843, the coastguards at East Prawle were responsible for watching the entire coast between Torcross and Salcombe. The coast was divided into 'guards', of two miles or so, each patrolled by a single coastguard. Today's coastal footpaths were worn by these men as they maintained their lonely night-time vigil.

In later years, white-washed or white quartzite stones were placed along the paths as a guide to the men patrolling on moonless nights. To ensure that the men covered their entire beat, letters would be exchanged with their opposite numbers at either end.

Old lookout on 'the Stroll' above Sharper's Head

The length of coast covered by the station was such that 'flying detachments' of two or three men were sent for a week to small lookout posts. The lookout at Gara Rock still survives and it is likely that the lookout at Prawle was first built for this purpose.

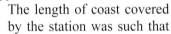

The old Lookout at Gara Rock

Although Punch magazine lampooned coastguard stations as 'castles of idleness, where able-bodied men spend their time looking through long glasses for imaginary smugglers', the reality was that coastguards were out on patrol, in all weathers, from dusk to dawn and in winter that could mean a sixteen hour turn of duty. Every day at dusk they assembled in the watch house, armed with pistol and cutlass or with musket and bayonet, and a blue light. Each man was allocated the guard of which he was to take charge, and off they marched to the shore where they patrolled

Coastguard Sentry 1831

until dawn. As the smugglers usually plied their trade on moonless nights, 'the darks' as they were called, it was usual to stand half the men down on the light nights of the full moon.

Because of the increased vigilance of the service, smugglers often adopted the practice of sinking their goods off the place where they planned to 'run' them. So, although the coastguards were usually off duty during the day, any word of a 'sinking' would mean the boats belonging to the station would be out 'creeping' and 'sweeping' for the goods. Creeping involved dragging an iron grapnel along the bottom, whilst sweeping was carried out by two boats rowed side-by-side with a rope dragged underwater between them.

For the coastguards, the hardships of the service and the hostility of local people were made tolerable by the prospect of prize money for a successful seizure of smuggled goods and 'blood money' for every smuggler taken and convicted. However, it was also bribes known as 'venturing money' that led many, in the early days of the service, to collude with the smugglers themselves.

Rickham Coastguard Station

In 1842 the Board of Customs agreed to build a new coastguard station at Rickham. This was on land, leased from a tenant of the Duke of Cleveland, at Long Gatter Field (the site of the later Gara Rock Hotel). A temporary station was in operation in 1843 but it was not until 1846 that the construction of the Rickham watch house, chief officer's house and six cottages, was completed. The 'Great Wall of Gara', a boundary wall protecting the exposed site from the sea, was built in the following year.

In addition to the Chief Officer, the crew of the station comprised the Chief Boatman, two Commissioned Boatmen and four Boatmen. When

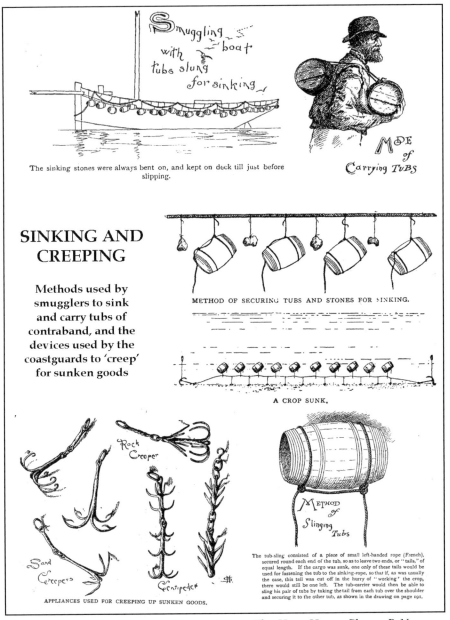

Source: *Smuggling Ways and Days*, Lieut. The Hon. Henry Shore, R.N., 1892

Rickham Coastguard Station, Gara Rock 1846-1909

Walter White visited the station in 1855, he was told that 'each man has to find his own clothes, and give five pounds a year rent for his house and garden, and he receives as pay a guinea a week, and an annual bonus of five pounds, equivalent to living rent free. "It isn't over much, but there's excitement in our life, hard as it is at times" '.

Ellen Luscombe in 1861, described Rickham as 'one of the loneliest spots imaginable. We heard terrible complaints of its dreariness from the gentleman in command. To be sure, the houses were duller than need be from being debarred by a wall from sight of the scenery, such protection from the high winds which blew from the sea being absolutely necessary. The men had a kind of burrow in the rock on which their flagstaff was fixed, to which they used to retire when on the look-out, but their families might as well live in a street for all they could see of the prospect'.

Sarah Fox visited the station in 1874 and described it more positively. 'The row of houses presents a neat and substantial appearance, and attached to each one is a well-cultivated little plot of garden ground. The rocket apparatus, for saving life from shipwrecks, occupies a detached building close to the flagstaff. From the look-out rock a fine sea view is obtained. ...Rickham was one of the Fitzroy storm-signal stations.' (The system of storm warning cones, hoisted whenever a gale was expected, was introduced by Vice-Admiral Robert Fitzroy in 1861 and was operated by many coastguard stations until 1981.)

Limebury Point Gun Battery

In 1845 new regulations required coastguards to undertake coast defence and, should the need arise, to serve on HM ships. Large calibre guns were placed at strategic locations and the coastguards trained in their use. By 1849 a battery had been built on Limebury Point commanding the entrance to Salcombe Harbour. The battery mounted one gun in 1849 and two by 1860. The stone walls of the battery magazine still stand at full height, under a dense growth of ivy, just above Limebury Point.

In June 1860 the Kingsbridge Gazette reported that 'coastguards from Salcombe and neighbourhood stations assembled at Rickham for practice with the large guns at the battery. The target of six feet square was placed about a half mile distant on the opposite side of the harbour (at Splat Cove), and 42 shots were fired at it. The firing was very accurate'.

Ellen Luscombe described the battery a few months later. 'Passing round the end of Limebury Point, we found a small shed containing a cannon and a few dozen of 36 pounder balls, to be used to defend the entrance of the harbour. I am afraid the *Jean Bart* or *La Gloire* would make light of them

if they came with hostile intent to the peaceful town. The preventive-men are required to practise a number of times in the year, and the reverberation of the cannon amongst the rocks is very fine, but it would not be pleasant to be walking there at the time, for the concussion must be fearful.'

(*Jean Bart* and *La Gloire* were powerful battleships in the French navy.)

A schooner about to cross the Bar c1910. The white building on Limebury Point was the magazine for the Limebury Point Gun Battery

6. FARMING AND FISHING, MILLING AND MINING

Historically, the threat of attack by invaders, raiders and pirates discouraged settlement near the shore and, consequently, human habitation was largely confined to inland locations on the plateau or in secluded wooded combes. Apart from the miller at Lower Lannacombe Mill (who, as we shall see, was himself the victim of a privateer's raid), the only occupants of the eight mile length of coastline between Start Point and Salcombe Bar, before the twentieth century, were men in uniform posted there to guard it: naval signalmen, lighthouse keepers and the men of the Preventive and Coastguard services. Nevertheless, local people, far from turning their back on the coast, have always been ready to exploit it.

Farming

Much of the coastal strip, below the plateau, is only suitable for rough grazing by hardy cattle, sheep and goats but, from at least the eighteenth century, arable farming has been carried out on those low terraces to the east of Prawle Point, formed as a result of changing sea levels. The Victorian travel writer Walter White described how the hills between Peartree and Prawle Points, 'sweep inwards from the shore, leaving a low, irregular plain, diversified by fields of grain and potatoes'. Here sand and seaweed were carried up from the beaches to fertilise the fields.

In more recent years, Prawle was renowned for the cauliflowers grown on these mild slopes facing the sea, the fields top dressed each spring with seaweed from Horseley Beach. A little to the east, the small fields either side of Maelcombe House were cultivated as a market garden, just after the First World War, by the Helby family and this continued to provide employment for local workers until the 1960s. Today, the slopes are grazed by prime beef cattle and sheep and, in places, cultivated for winter feedcrops.

To the west of Prawle Point, arable farming was, and still is, largely confined to the higher plateau slopes. At Rickham Common the medieval open field system survived, in the form of 141 thin strips, until at least 1874.

Fishing

Although fishing has always been carried out by the local population, the lack of safe anchorages has generally limited it to a seasonal, part-time activity. At Prawle, fishermen had to make the most of rocky inlets such as Landing Cove just to the east of Prawle Point. In 1851 Walter White

The fishermen of Ivy Cove, Lannacombe before and after World War II
(Photos: Bill Login, Richard Partridge)

described Landing Cove as 'a port in miniature – a small basin in which some half-dozen fishing boats may float, surrounded by rocks, with no outlet but a narrow groove worn through the reef. Notwithstanding the contracted entrance, which must necessitate delicate steering, the fishermen use it as a harbour; and in the hollows of the big rock close by they find store-rooms for their tackle and vaults

Landing Cove with the Prawle Point Coastguard Cottages above on the left

for their fish'. The metal eyes that secured their store-pots can still be seen leaded into the rocks.

In Lannacombe Bay, evidence of fishing from Woodcombe and Ivy Coves can be found in medieval manorial records. In the reign of Richard II (1377-99) Woodcombe's five farming tenants all paid an annual rent of one shilling for sea fishing rights. At Ivy Cove, just to the east of Woodcombe, rent was paid for a cellar called a 'botehouse' during the reign of Henry VII (1485-1509).

Around 1880 there were eleven fishermen working from Ivy Cove and Landing Cove mostly during the summer. Their mainstay was crab fishing. Working in pairs, the men sailed and rowed their small open boats to set and lift their pots. The boats were similar to the Hallsands crabbers – beamy, clinker built, open beach boats – but they tended to be of heavier construction because of the rockier shore west of the Start. In winter, the men trapped rabbits, worked on farms and repaired their ink-well crabpots with willow grown in nearby groves.

At Lannacombe the beach was not suitable for netting the fish required to bait their pots and so the Lannacombe men worked alongside their Hallsands neighbours in manning the seine boats and gear. After the village of Hallsands was destroyed in a storm in 1917 a number of the fishermen moved away. In 1922 William Login moved with two sons, John and Frank, to Lannacombe and first rented, but later bought, the old Coastguard houses at Ivy Cove from the Admiralty. His other three sons went to East Prawle but all fished out of Ivy Cove. Several Prawle fishermen also moved their boats there so that, before the Second World War, there were at least five boats working out of Ivy Cove. By this time sail and oar had given way to the open inboard motor boat.

There was a drastic decline after the War in small boat fishery and by 1960 there were only two working boats left at Lannacombe. Large purpose-built crab boats were introduced at that time and in 1969 commercial fishing from Lannacombe ended when one pair of fishermen went to Dartmouth and the other to Salcombe, where the new boats were berthed.

Milling

Corn mills were built beside the stream at Lannacombe in medieval times and continued working until the nineteenth century. Higher Lannacombe Mill was about a mile inland and, just below it, a leat was taken off the stream to feed a mill at Lower Lannacombe. Just visible, near Lannacombe Farm, are the ruins of an overshot watermill on the cliff above the beach, as well as two millstones beside the coast path. Still working in 1803, the mill was in ruins when the 1847 tithe map was drawn.

There is a story attached to the old mill-house at Lannacombe Cove. During the Napoleonic Wars a French privateer raided the coast at night and stripped the miller of all his goods – even taking his bed. The miller, having by him a considerable sum of money in a purse, flung it out of the window.

At daybreak there was no trace of the privateer and, searching in his garden, he had the good fortune to see his purse with all its contents hanging in an elder tree. The tree was preserved for many years as 'the tree which saved the miller's money' but sadly no trace of it remains today.

Adjacent to the mill complex at Lower Lannacombe was a limekiln, built in the late 18th or early 19th century.

Coal and limestone would have been brought in by boat and burnt in layers in the kiln to produce lime for soil improvement and for mortar.

Lannacombe Beach and Lannacombe Farm. The limekiln was incorporated into the later building

Mining

Deckler's Cliff

Sarah Fox, in her account of a visit to Rickham Coastguard Station in 1874, referred to iron mines having been 'lately worked there'. Evidence of these workings can still be seen today. Ruins of what is believed to be a smiths' workshop remain in the small combe just above Seacombe Sand and, on Deckler's or Dictor's Island to the east, a stone lined chute for the ore, metal stakes for an inclined railway and the postholes for a quay platform and crane are all visible. On 13 November 1858, the Kingsbridge Gazette reported that 'the iron mine lately opened on Dictor's Island is turning out well. About 100 tons of ore have been brought in from the mine and landed on Mr. Lakeman's Quay. Buildings are in

Ruins of a building, possibly a smithy, above Seacombe Sand

Deckler's or Dictor's Island, east of Gara Rock

31

process of erection on the sett for smiths' shops etc.'

Pits, adits and dumps were created on Deckler's Cliff and 'a tramway zig-zagged down onto Deckler's Island, where iron ore was tipped from the trucks down a stone chute onto a quay below. Ore was stored on platforms on the south side of the island before being shipped, and an inclined railway constructed of timber, which climbed the west side of the island, brought materials up to the mine' (*Robert Waterhouse*). The mine did not prosper, however. On 6 February 1858 the Plymouth smack *Hope* bound for Deckler's Island for a cargo of iron ore was driven ashore near Prawle Point. It was not expected that she would get off again, but the vessel was eventually re-floated on 16 June. In 1858, the

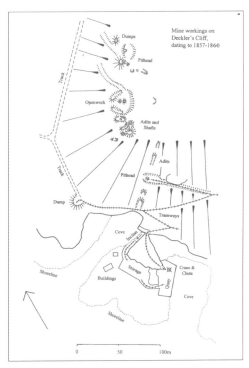

Plan of the Deckler's Cliff mine workings (Robert Waterhouse)

mine produced 54 tons of iron ore valued at just under £30. No detailed returns were made thereafter and production was suspended by 1863.

East Prawle Iron Mine

In its edition of 5 February 1857, the Exeter Flying Post reported that 'there is a prospect of an iron mine being worked shortly at East Prawle. A party of practical men examined the place and state it as their opinion that it will turn out a profitable investment. Iron is found in abundance in the surface of the rocks on the edge of the cliff and it is also generally supposed that lead and silver may be found there. Already several houses have been taken on for those who are engaged to commence operations, which they will do so shortly'. A sale of 300 tons of iron ore for £142 was reported in 1858 but no further reports were issued and it is probable that the mine was abandoned during the depression of the iron trade in 1859-60.

There is some doubt as to the precise location of the mine. At Pig's Nose near Moor Sand there are the remains of an openwork or small quarry, the site of a building and also an adit, about 17 metres in length. Whether this was the East Prawle Iron mine or part of the Deckler's Cliff workings is a matter of conjecture.

Some sources identify Maceley Cove to the east as the East Prawle site. Reference is made to small iron lodes, as well as banks, walls, converging tracks, and a platform at the top of the cliff and what may be a spoil heap in Maceley Cove, but the latter could equally well be erosion debris.

Exploratory works may have taken place there, but in 1861, according to Ellen Luscombe, it was not iron ore but sand that was being exploited when she visited Maceley Cove. 'This little cove was frequented by people from a considerable

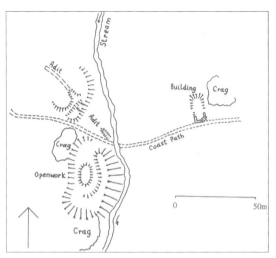

Plan of the Pig's Nose Iron Workings (Robert Waterhouse)

Remains of Iron Workings at Pig's Nose near Moor Sand

distance for the sake of the beautiful white sand, which is so scarce an article on that coast; but it could only be brought to the top by donkeys, and it was wonderful to see how the poor creatures picked their way round the projecting pieces of rock which rendered the path so difficult, never stumbling.' Above the cliff an old trackway, leading inland, is still known as the Donkey Path.

7. SAVING LIFE AT SEA IN VICTORIAN TIMES

Start Point Lighthouse

The years following the end of the Napoleonic Wars saw a dramatic rise in sea trade and, with it, a tragic increase in the number of shipwrecks along the South Devon coast. Particularly notorious were the rocks and shoals off Start Point and so in 1833 Trinity House instructed its consultant engineer, James Walker, to come up with plans for a lighthouse on or near Start Point. On 1 July

Start Point Lighthouse completed in 1836 (Trinity House)

1836, one year before Queen Victoria came to the throne, the lighthouse was illuminated for the first time. It had taken two years to build and cost £5,892. Today the lighthouse still shines its guiding light for the benefit of mariners as they make their way up and down channel. The full story of the lighthouse is set out in the author's book *Start Point and Its Lighthouse*.

Coastguard Rescue

In spite of its many shortcomings, the Coastguard service was, by the 1850s, beginning to win the war against smugglers, albeit largely because the abolition of tariffs on many items made the trade less profitable. As a result the role of the service was about to change. The outset of the Crimean War in 1854 saw 3,000 coastguards serving aboard naval vessels. (At Rickham all the able-bodied men under fifty had been called up for service, with their places partly filled by pensioners.) However, their lack of sea training caused much criticism, to which the Admiralty responded by calling for control of the service. This was put into effect by the Coast Guard

Service Act of 1856, which defined the new duties as *firstly*, the defence of the coast, *secondly*, the manning of HM ships in time of war and *thirdly*, the protection of the Revenue. The last became a minor duty and, until the outbreak of the Great War, the Coastguard was primarily a coast defence force.

In this new role the Coastguard gradually gave more emphasis to 'assisting vessels in danger, taking charge of wrecks, the operation of life-saving apparatus and participating in lifeboat rescues'. Although the Society for the Preservation of Life from Shipwreck (later the RNLI) had been formed in 1824, there was no lifeboat on the South Hams coast until 1869 when the Salcombe station at South Sands was established. Shore-based life-saving apparatus was also late in coming to the area, in spite of the high number of shipwrecks. In 1851 only Torcross and Challaborough coastguard stations were equipped with a mortar lifesaving appliance. This had been developed by George Manby at Great Yarmouth in 1807 and could fire a shot, with 500

yards of line, from the shore to a wrecked ship. The line and the hawser attached to it were then hauled in by the shipwrecked crew and used to bring them ashore in a travelling cot (the forerunner of the breeches buoy).

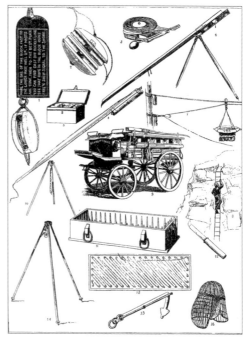

Meanwhile, potentially more effective and more portable rocket-based systems were being developed and, by 1865, the mortar had largely been replaced by the rocket device developed by Captain Edward Boxer. Attached to the rocket was a continuous length of line (of Italian hemp) from a flaking-box in which the line was coiled over a series of pins. The 500 yard line or whip was the means of passing a heavier line, the hawser. This was used in conjunction with the Kisbee Sling Life-buoy, a circular

The Board of Trade Rocket Apparatus

cork life-buoy from which was suspended a pair of canvas breeches. The reliability of the Boxer system meant that it became the standard equipment right up to 1948 when it was replaced by the Rescue Rocket. By 1874 the Board of Trade had supplied the rocket apparatus to 300 coastguard stations.

Each station kept a cart which was stocked with tripod, lights, rockets, ropes and other essentials. Local volunteers formed a rescue team to assist the coastguards and each member was allocated a number denoting a specific duty. Trained by station officers, they were timed by inspecting officers on random visits. The cart and apparatus were housed in purpose-built 'rocket houses', many of which remain today.

At East Prawle, the former rocket house, built in 1870, still stands below the old coastguard cottages at Seaview at the bottom of Newhouses Hill. The East Prawle Lifesaving Apparatus Company was formed in 1878 and for one hundred years was to do sterling service, until the rocket apparatus was with-drawn in 1979.

The Rocket House at East Prawle

In these days of dramatic helicopter rescues, it is easy to forget the part that shore-based rescue teams played in saving numerous lives along our coast.

Gossamer 1868

The first account of the rocket apparatus being used on this coast was in 1868 when the 734 ton clipper, *Gossamer* of Liverpool, bound from London to Adelaide, went ashore at Landing Cove, to the east of Prawle Point on Thursday, 10 December 1868.

Coming down channel with a pilot on board, the *Gossamer* had run into a strong SSW gale off Start Point. Captain Thomson, believing that the ship would weather Prawle Point, went below to his newly-wed wife in the cabin. The pilot, Andrew Grant, assumed command and ordered chief officer Merrifield to set more sail.

When Captain Thomson finally came back on deck all was confusion, with all three officers giving orders. With Prawle Point just half a mile off to the west, the pilot put the helm hard down. But it was too late, the ship swung head to wind, and at 2.15pm the *Gossamer* struck the rocks near Landing Cove. Heavy seas prevented the crew from launching the boats.

James Pengelly, the chief officer at Prawle Coastguard Station turned out his men and sent to Rickham for the rocket apparatus. Lieutenant Smyth at Rickham station was quick to respond, but his station was two miles away and much valuable time was lost.

Some of the crew jumped overboard to swim ashore but most perished in the attempt. The captain and his young wife were on deck in 'an agony of distress'. Shortly after her husband had tied a lifebelt to her, Mrs. Thomson was washed overboard by a large wave. The captain jumped after her, but her lifebelt had come off and the back tow of the wave swept them both seawards. Two hours later their bodies came ashore together.

Six of the crew were brought ashore by means of the rocket apparatus, whilst some of the swimmers were saved by rescuers – fishermen and coastguards – who formed a human chain to pull them out of the water to safety.

The gravestone in Chivelstone churchyard of Gossamer's captain and his wife

As the tide fell, rescuers managed to get aboard the wreck where they saved two more lives. One, the cook, refused to leave and had to be taken off by force. The second, a doctor, had lashed himself to the rail, and was virtually unconscious at the time of his rescue. Of the 31 passengers and crew, 19 were saved and were taken to the Union and Providence Inns in East Prawle.

Next day the ship broke up and the cargo, which consisted chiefly of shop goods, was strewn along the coast. Word quickly spread and, within hours, hundreds of people descended on the scene. 'The neighbourhood of Prawle Point presented an exceedingly animated appearance. The bulk of the cargo lay near the wreck, scores of the packing cases being unbroken, and there the coastguardmen and a body of police kept efficient watch, but it would have required a small army to have guarded the miles of coast along which property was washing ashore...Wherever there was a chance of "wrecking" the "wreckers" gathered, and the beach could be seen dotted by hundreds, whilst the country lanes near Prawle were quite lively with the traffic.'

A month after the *Gossamer* struck, the scene of the wreck 'viewed from the top of the cliff, resembled a large military encampment. On Tuesday and the following days, the whole of the goods were put to the hammer, and the auction attracted a congregation of not less than a thousand people'.

Emilie 1870

On the night of 29 May 1870, sailing up-channel in thick fog, the German barque *Emilie*, carrying nitrate of soda from Chile to Germany, struck the rocks just to the west of Prawle Point. The crew took to their boats, and pulled off clear of the land. By daylight the fog had cleared and the boats were seen by Prawle coastguards. Mr. Murray, the chief officer, launched his boat, and brought the thirteen-man crew to Prawle. The vessel broke up in a few hours, and the wreck was washed along the shore for several miles. Very little of value could be recovered as the cargo had dissolved.

Lalla Rookh 1873

The rocket life-saving apparatus in action

The first time that the new rocket life-saving apparatus at East Prawle was used to save lives was on the morning of Monday, 3 March 1873, when fifteen men from the 869 ton tea clipper *Lalla Rookh* of Liverpool were saved off Gammon Head. The *Lalla Rookh*, a fine iron vessel commanded by Captain Fullerton, was on her way to London from Shanghai with a cargo of tea and tobacco, when she encountered thick fog in the Channel and at 5.45am, she struck the rocks at

The tea clipper Lalla Rookh
wrecked in Maceley Cove, 1873

Gammon Head, while in full sail.

Anchors were let go at once, but, lifted by the waves, the ship drifted into Maceley Cove. Four of the crew saved themselves by jumping onto the rocks. At the same time a boat was lowered and five men jumped in, but it capsized immediately. The mate was drowned but the other four men managed to clamber back aboard the ship.

One of the Rickham coastguards had seen the ship coming onto the rocks and ran back to the Rickham station for the rocket apparatus. But it was the Prawle coastguards who were to get there first. One of the crew who had climbed up the rocks had made his way to Prawle to summon help. Chief Officer John Segrue called out his men and the rocket apparatus was taken the one and a half miles to the cliffs above the cove. The first line fell across the ship and, with the coastguards 'working the apparatus with a hearty goodwill', the fifteen men were brought ashore within twenty-five minutes .

The ship held together, settling down into the sand, but on the Tuesday evening she broke amidships. Some of the tea chests were salvaged, but large quantities of tea, from broken chests, washed up on to the beach, lining the shore at high water mark. It is said that Prawle folk quickly developed a taste for salt in their tea!

Utility 1877

In the early hours of 9 January 1877, five men were rescued by the Prawle Rocket Team from the stricken 90 ton schooner *Utility* of Fleetwood, bound for Runcorn with a cargo of stone and caught in thick fog and a sou'westerly gale. A watchman at Prawle Coastguard Station had seen the vessel running into danger and had shone his blue light as a warning, but it was to no avail as *Utility* struck on a reef of flat rocks some distance from the shore.

The rocket apparatus was soon brought up and three rockets were fired before the line was got on board. However, the five-man crew did not know how to attach the hawser and it was a long time before they were all landed. The *Western Morning News* commented: 'with regard to the crews' ignorance of the manner of working the rocket lines it is to be regretted that the owners do not more generally accept the offer of the Board of Trade to supply free of charge enamel plates containing instructions as to their use'.

Pauline 1877

Charles Harris, the Chief Officer at Rickham, and two of his men were on watch in the lookout on the night of 14 October 1877 when the French brig-antine *Pauline* struck Gaytor (Gara) Rock below them. The *Pauline*, with a crew of eight and a cargo of figs and almonds, was sailing to Dunkirk when she was caught in a heavy gale. She was showing no lights and Harris and his colleagues were unaware of the wreck until remains of the ship were found on Rickham Sand the following morning. At daylight they made a search of the beach, but could not find anyone alive. The ship's headboard, with the name *Pauline*, was found and later that day fishermen found the bodies of seven of the crew – another was later washed ashore. Six of the men, including the captain, were buried at East Portlemouth church.

Meirion 1879

On the morning of Sunday, 7 September 1879, the *Meirion* of Liverpool, an iron-built three-masted brigantine of about 1,400 tons, came ashore on the same spot where the *Pauline* had been wrecked nearly two years earlier. The year-old *Meirion*, home-ward bound from Rangoon with a cargo of rice, was commanded by Captain Wil-liams and had a crew of 21. Encountering fog coming up channel the captain was unaware of his position when land was sighted. Several attempts were made to put the ship about but, missing stays, she came ashore at 2.30am, very near low tide. The coast-guards at Rickham sent off a

The Meirion wrecked below Gara Rock, 1879

rocket line as soon as they saw the vessel was in danger. The captain, how-ever, had the line thrown overboard, shouting at the same time, 'We don't want that, we want a tug'. A boat was lowered from the *Meirion* and the captain and six of his men went off to Salcombe, and after much delay arranged for the *Sir Walter Raleigh* of Plymouth to tow her off. But it was too late, high tides had driven the vessel onto the rocks and, as darkness was drawing in, the captain, having returned to his ship, came off with sixteen of the crew by means of the previously despised rocket-line. Only 120 tons of the *Meirion's* cargo of 2,000 tons were salvaged. At the subsequent Board of Trade inquiry Captain Williams was blamed for the loss of his ship and had his master's certificate suspended for six months.

Eugene 1880

Six months later another ship, the French schooner *Eugene*, was wrecked, with tragic consequences, in almost the same location. At 8am, 16 February 1880, the coastguards at Rickham observed a schooner about two miles off, drifting in a force nine south-westerly gale. Her mainmast was gone, her foremast broken and, with the wreckage hanging over her side, the sea was breaking completely over her. A man was seen on board waving his hat for assistance. Two hours later the vessel drifted within fifty yards of the shore, directly under the coastguard station. The rocket apparatus was brought into action and fired from the cliffs, under the direction of John Segrue, the chief officer. The man on the schooner caught the line but, just as he was hauling it in, a heavy sea knocked him overboard. Two coastguards, McClements and Keats, climbed down to a gully and pulled him in by the rocket line but, as McClements reached out to grab the man, a wave broke over them and washed both coastguards into the sea. Keats, still holding onto the line was rescued, but McClements and the man were swept away.

Next day the body of the man was found in a bay below Rickham Common. He was later identified as Captain Volante. The mutilated body of 35 year old David McClements was found in Fairslade's Cove four days later. Only a few weeks before, McClements had lost his wife and a child and, as a result of this tragedy, his remaining five year old daughter was orphaned. He was buried in Stokenham churchyard beside his wife.

Glad Tidings 1882

The coast between Rickham and Prawle has been the scene of many avoidable shipping disasters. Over-confident and, on occasion, incompetent masters have, all too often, failed to allow sufficient sea-room when making passage along a lee shore. Some have been too ready to make assumptions about their position when making a landfall, with Bolt Head being mistaken for Prawle and Prawle for Start – excusable perhaps in thick fog but grossly negligent otherwise. Captain McMullen, master of a fine full-rigged ship, the 1,300 ton *Glad Tidings* of St. Johns, New Brunswick, was in the over-confident category. He had left Calcutta on 10 August 1882 with a crew of twenty hands and a cargo of 1,800 tons of linseed in bags. Bound up-channel on the evening of 15 December, with a stiff SSW breeze, the lookout saw land to their lee and the captain was called. It was Bolt Head that had been sighted, but Captain McMullen judged it to be Prawle Point and did not think it necessary to take soundings. Coming on deck ten minutes later he saw land close under the lee bow. He ordered the helm to be put hard down and called all hands to 'bout ship', but it was too late and the ship struck

Maceley Cove with Gammon Head on the right

the rocks amidships at the entrance to Maceley Cove, where the *Lalla Rookh* had been wrecked nine years earlier.

It was now just after eleven o'clock at night. Efforts were made to get out the boats without success. So, to ease the ship, orders were given to cut away the rigging but when the main mast fell it stove in the two boats aft. Brave attempts were then made, in turn, by three of the crew to swim ashore with a line. Two of the men were dashed back against the vessel's side by the waves and were hauled aboard in a state of exhaustion. The third attempt by a Finn ended in disaster when the rope attached to his body parted in the heavy surf and he was swept out to sea.

Meanwhile oakum soaked in paraffin, and then bedding, were burnt to attract help from ashore. However, the paraffin must have leaked, for flames soon came bursting up through the poop deck. The fire raged fiercely, cutting off communication between the two ends of the vessel. Trapped forward were the first mate and five men, and in the small space aft, were the captain and the remainder of the crew. All now faced the terrible prospect of either drowning or being burnt alive.

Fortunately the reflection of the fire had been spotted, soon after midnight, by a duty coastguard at Rickham. He made his way to the top of Gammon Head and at 1am saw the wreck below. Leaving a blue light burning on the ground, to indicate that help was on its way, he rushed back to Rickham and reported to his chief, John Moore. Moore promptly sent one of his men, Henry Sivyer, to Salcombe to notify the divisional commander and another man to get the horses to take the rocket apparatus to Gammon Head. In spite of the haste, the coastguards and the cart drawn by three horses did not arrive at the cliffs above the wreck until 2.45am. Meanwhile Sivyer, having delivered his message to Salcombe, had got there before them.

When the men at the stern of the burning ship saw Sivyer, they attempted to throw a lead line to him. Wading out into the surf, he caught the line and made it fast to a rock. Three men, including Captain McMullen, then made their way, hand over hand, to the shore. Another man lost his grip whilst midway across the rope, dropped into the surf and was washed away. Shortly afterwards the rocket apparatus was brought into action and a line put across to the six men at the bow. They were lucky to come ashore uninjured. The low-lying rocks, from which the apparatus was worked, were swamped by breaking waves and each man was dragged through the surging water amidst floating spars.

It was four o'clock before all of the nineteen survivors were brought ashore. They were then sent up to the Union Inn in Prawle. Curiously enough one of them, Richard White, was among those saved from the *Lalla Rookh*. During all the time the crew were being landed the fire continued to burn fiercely and by mid-morning the ship was broken in two and the whole coast strewn with wreckage.

Reliance 1888

The paddle steamer *Reliance*, a 31 ton tug, built in 1874 on the Isle of Wight, was being towed down channel by another tug, the *Conqueror*, on 30 December 1888 when she sprang a leak. Abandoned by her four-man crew she foundered off Gammon Head, where her paddlewheels, boilers and engines now lie in a deep gully.

Sunk off Gammon Head in 1888, the steam tug Reliance

Marana 1891

On one terrible night in 1891 as many as 52 seamen were lost when four ships were dashed onto the rocks around Start Point, victims of one of the most violent storms ever recorded on the coast of South Devon – the Great Blizzard of 9-10 March 1891. The north-easterly winds reached up to hurricane force, whilst driving snowstorms reduced visibility to a matter of yards. Twenty five of those lost were from the 2,177 ton schooner-rigged steamer, *Marana* of Liverpool, which was bound from London to Ceylon (now Sri Lanka) with a cargo of railway sleepers.

Between five and six o'clock in the evening of Monday, 9 March 1891 *Marana* struck the Black Stone Rock just below Start Point. The engines had been at full speed but stopped with the force of the impact. Captain Frigginson was on the bridge and ordered the 27 crew to abandon ship. There was no panic. As the starboard lifeboat pushed off with 22 of the men, the Captain called out 'Be careful lads, and keep off the shore. I am afraid you will all be drowned'. Soon afterwards Captain Frigginson, the three mates, the chief engineer and the steward got into a small boat. They were never seen again.

The coastguards at Hallsands had been informed of the wreck of the *Marana* at 6.45pm by a messenger sent by the lighthouse keeper. They immediately despatched a messenger to Prawle, five miles away, for the life-saving apparatus. He arrived at Prawle Coastguard Station at 7.30pm, and about eight o'clock the apparatus left for Start Point in charge of the Chief Officer, William Hewett, with six coastguards and eleven men of the Volunteer Life Saving Company. When they arrived at Start Farm, they were told that the steamship had broken up five minutes after she struck. As it was assumed that the crew had all been drowned, they were told to proceed to Beesands, to rescue the crew of the schooner *Lunesdale* that had gone on shore there.

Ignoring their captain's advice, the 22 men in *Marana's* lifeboat attempted to land at Horseley Cove to the west, but there was a heavy surf breaking on the shore and, as they turned, the boat capsized. Only twelve of them were able to regain the boat and get hold of the keel. After a time the boat was righted, but she was full of water. Those that remained clung to the gunwales as the boat drifted towards the Meg Rock, off Langerstone Point. Almost immediately the boat struck rocks and was smashed to pieces; only five men reached the shore.

Four of the men, all Swedes and all firemen on the *Marana*, came ashore together, unaware of the fifth. All were exhausted, but one of them, Edward Rasmussen, was in a particularly wretched state. He had injured his back on the rocks and had lost his boots and most of his clothes. Carrying Rasmussen between them, his crewmates struggled over the cliffs into the fields. Unable to carry him further, they found shelter in a furze brake. Two stayed with Rasmussen, trying to keep him alive, whilst the third, Gustav Anderson, went in search of help. It was ten o'clock when he reached a cottage near the coastguard buildings. Albert Rich, the only coastguard remaining at the station and John Perry, a Lloyd's signalman, were summoned but, as the young Swede spoke very little English, they were unable to establish what had become of his crewmates. So, leaving him behind, they started to search near Horseley Cove.

Meanwhile two of the coastguards who had gone to Start Farm were sent back and, meeting up with Rich and Perry, joined the search, this time to the westward as far as Copstone Cove below Prawle Point. They then turned back to Langerstone Point. Seeing their blue light, the two men who had stayed with Rasmussen, came rushing down to meet them. It was now 2.30am on Tuesday morning and the conditions were dreadful, with hurricane force winds and blinding snow. The coastguards were guided to the place where Rasmussen lay but, finding him already dead, the two Swedes were taken to the station having been out in the snow for over six hours. The coastguards and villagers at Prawle did all they could for the three survivors and supplied them with warm clothing. They were later taken to Salcombe, where they were clothed by the Shipwrecked Mariners' Society and sent to London.

The bodies of seven of *Marana's* crew were washed on shore at Prawle, very near to where the lifeboat capsized, on the Wednesday following the wreck. A week later the body of the fifth man that had come ashore was found in the snow just 100 yards away from where his crewmate Rasmussen had met a similar fate.

Theckla **1891**

On 23 April 1891, six weeks after the loss of the *Marana*, the 378 ton Swedish barque *Theckla*, carrying timber to Plymouth, had her rudder damaged by heavy seas near Start Point. The vessel quickly became unmanageable and her master, Captain Everson, decided to beach her. The Prawle coastguards, seeing that she would come ashore, signalled her crew to run for Horseley Cove. The coastguards got a rocket line across her, but the ten-man crew, not knowing how to work the apparatus, took to their boat and came safely ashore. Tugs were summoned from Plymouth, but the *Theckla* was carried onto rocks with the rising tide, so the coastguards assisted the crew in salvaging all that could be taken off.

SS Maria 1892

During a dense fog on the morning of 26 June 1892, the 1,655 ton Greek steamer *Maria*, bound for Rotterdam with a cargo of grain, ran onto Langler Rocks on the west side of Prawle Point. Both Salcombe lifeboat and coastguard boat turned out, but the 23-man crew were able to get ashore in their own boats. The steel vessel was only a year old. Much of the grain was taken off by barge

SS Maria on Langler Rocks, Prawle Point 1892

but the vessel broke up in heavy seas on 19 July and hopes of salvaging her were abandoned. One hundred years later in 1992, the cargo ship *Demetrios* was wrecked in the same location.

Franchise 1897

The Belfast brigantine *Franchise*, carrying coal from Cardiff to Littlehampton, was beating up channel just after midnight on 6 November 1897 when, coming too far in towards the land, she was driven ashore about half a mile east of Prawle Point. The duty coastguard, seeing in the moonlight a ship stranded in Dutch Pool below Sharper's Head, called his colleagues and together they boarded her and offered assistance. The crew remained on board for some hours but, unable to save her, came off in their boat. Tugs were called but, by the time they arrived, the vessel was driven onto rocks at high tide. She broke up during the course of the following week.

8. MAYHEM AND BLOODSHED IN EAST PRAWLE 1872

The most macabre incident to occur along this coast, in Victorian times, was in 1872, when a seaman from a wrecked Italian sailing ship, the **Maria Theresa,** ran amok in East Prawle, wounding six people with a knife before he was finally slain by a coastguard officer.

The Pig's Nose Inn, East Prawle, formerly the Union Inn

In the early hours of Thursday, 4 December 1872, the brig *Maria Theresa*, bound from Shields for Genoa, with a cargo of coals, was damaged in a collision with a vessel off Start Point. Her master, Nicholo Bozzo, ran her on shore near Prawle to prevent her sinking. After she struck, he and the crew were able to get ashore and were taken to the Union Inn.

A telegram was then sent to Hingston & Sons, Lloyd's agents and Italian consuls at Dartmouth, who sent their employee, George Browne, an Italian speaker, to Prawle. Arriving at 3.30pm that Thursday, he met the captain and mate. Later that evening Browne sent a man to see if the ship was breaking up and, finding it was, he and the Italians all went down to see what they could save. Captain Bozzo ordered the men to stay there for the night, but five of them disobeyed him by returning to the Inn. Bozzo, and the rest of his crew, remained with the stricken ship until the morning. One of those who had defied the Captain was a 38 year old Sicilian, Salvatore Hari. Hari, an able seaman, had been with Captain Bozzo for about five months, and they had had frequent quarrels. All the crew were afraid of him.

Before retiring to his room that night, George Browne saw that the Italians were all in bed, but just after two o'clock in the morning he heard a loud noise coming from their room. The Sicilian was attacking his crewmates, striking them with his fists. Freeing themselves, the men ran out of the house, and into the stable. Later they heard Hari go past, calling out that if he caught them he would drink their blood.

John Patey, the landlord, also awakened by the noise, was asked by Browne to call the police but, when told that there was none in the village, he asked Patey to call the coastguard instead. Down at the Coastguard station Patey threw stones at the windows of the Chief Officer's house and, when John Segrue appeared, Patey urged him to come with his men to the village, saying that some of the foreign men were murdering each other.

When Segrue arrived at the Union Inn with two of his men, Colwell and Wilcocks, he asked Browne to go up with him and speak to the Italians. Segrue went in front with his cutlass drawn. Browne and Colwell followed and Patey, the landlord, was behind with a candle. As they went up the stairs Hari sprang onto the landing, holding a knife. Browne said, in Italian, 'Boy, in the name of God give up that knife and go to bed'. With that Hari attempted to stab him. Segrue caught him by the hand but in the scuffle the candle went out. Hari then ran out of the door, pursued by Colwell. In a few minutes Colwell came back, with blood on his head, saying he had been stabbed. A search was then mounted for Hari in the direction of the Coast-guard station. Segrue had his cutlass, Wilcocks his tuck stick and Browne, a pistol, whilst Patey carried a lantern.

Hari had already made his way down to the Coastguard station. On his way he met Mrs. Colwell, who was coming up to see what the alarm was about. Hari rushed at her, stabbed her several times, and then went on down to the coastguard houses. Seeing a light at the window of James Brown's cottage, he tapped on the window. Brown opened the door and was immediately attacked. The Italian repeat-edly stabbed him, even after he had fallen to the ground. Hari then turned, in a frenzy, on Mrs. Brown wounding her in the head and hands.

A Coastguard's tuck stick used by boarding parties to prod for contraband cargo

Her son, Thomas Brown, a powerfully built young man, was awoken by his mother shouting 'Murder!' He came down and stood between them. Hari struck at him with his knife but Brown caught the Italian round the waist, and threw him over the wall. Finding his father lying badly wounded in the officers' yard, he took him up and carried him home, after which he saw Hari looking through the window, shaking his knife.

A little later, Segrue, Wilcocks, Browne, and Patey met Mrs. Colwell after leaving the inn. Between screams, she told them that she had been badly wounded by one of the sailors who was now down at the coastguard buildings stabbing everyone he could find. The party went on down the lane until they reached Mr. John Sture's gate, where there was a recess in the wall. It was here that Hari sprang out at Segrue, and attempted to stab him in the chest, the knife striking a button. He made another attempt when Segrue touched him with the point of the cutlass, which made him even wilder than before. Hari took one step backwards, and with a yell he rushed at Segrue but, before he had time to strike, Segrue cut him with a backhand stroke on the forehead. Hari fell on his knees, still grasping his knife. Wilcocks, with his tuck stick drawn, jumped in and held him down. Segrue dropped the cutlass and closed with Hari, taking the knife from him. It was at this point that Hari fell on Wilcocks' tuck stick. He died soon after.

The Coroner's Inquest into Hari's death was held the following day at the Union Inn. The Coroner, Mr. Michelmore, in summing up, said that Hari had died from the wound in the back, as a result of the blow given by Wilcocks. The fact that he was a coastguard did not alter the case, for coastguards were not bound to keep the peace whenever called upon. The Jury, after a short deliberation, found 'that though the two coastguardsmen, Wilcocks and Segrue, exceeded their duty, yet morally they considered that they had done their duty, and that the deceased died from a wound given by Wilcocks acciden- tally, whilst attempting to disarm the man'.

The people of Prawle did reap one benefit from this unhappy episode. Three hundred tons of the 'very best Sunderland coals' were washed up from the wreck of the *Maria Theresa* and were bought at auction by local folk at a knock down price. Plymouth buyers bought the hull and rigging.

The old coastguard cottages at Seaview where the Italian sailor made a frenzied attack on coastguard James Brown and his wife

The scenes of this tragic affair: the Pig's Nose Inn, the old coastguard buildings at Seaview and the place in Newhouses Hill where Hari was finally silenced, can all be seen today. Local farmer, Derek Wotton, recalls that, as a child in Prawle nearly seventy years ago, he and the other children in the village, were always frightened of going past the spot in the lane near Shepherd's Farm, where the 'mad Italian' had been slain by the coastguards.

9. PRAWLE SIGNAL STATIONS 1868-1913

Sir William Mitchell's Signal Station 1868-83

Before the advent of ship-to-shore radio telegraphy in the twentieth century, ship-owners found it difficult to keep track of their vessels once they had sailed out of port. However, with the establishment of signal stations on prominent headlands from the 1850s, the masters of ships could at least report their position by closing the headland and signalling their identity and intentions using semaphore or flags. The signal station, connected by telegraph to London, would then report the vessel and, if it was homeward bound, shipping agents were then able to make advance arrangements for berthing, sale of cargo etc., thereby reducing turn-round times. Messages from owners or agents could also be passed from shore to ship, informing the master of his next port of call to load or unload a cargo, so avoiding the need to put into an intermediate port for orders.

Most of the early signal stations were established by Lloyd's of London who published shipping movements in Lloyd's List (the first Lloyd's station was established at Deal in 1852). However, it was a rival of Lloyds, Sir William Mitchell, owner of the *Shipping Gazette,* who established the first commercial signal station at Prawle in 1868.

Sir William obtained permission to place a flagstaff in a field above the Coastguard station at Seaview, East Prawle, and also for the Coastguard to take signals for him. The United Kingdom Telegraph Co. connected the Coastguard station with Kingsbridge shortly afterwards. On 15 February 1868, the *Kingsbridge Gazette* reported that 'the line of telegraph to Prawle was opened on Monday, and now the masters of any vessels, outward or homeward bound, will be able to report themselves speedily, on one condition – that they use the Commercial code in signalling'.

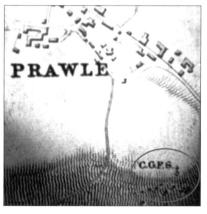

The site of Sir William Mitchell's Signal Station shown as C.G.F.S. on a Victorian Admiralty Chart

The *Commercial Code,* afterwards known as the *International Code,* was a signal book, produced in 1857, for use by merchant vessels of all nations. It enabled a vessel to identify herself by a hoist of four signal flags, for

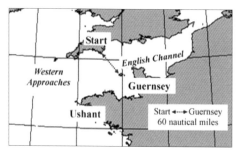

The signal stations at Prawle were close to Start Point, an important landfall for ships coming up-channel

example the Salcombe schooner *Huntress* was allocated the signal letters 'UCGL'. The International Code of Signals is still in use today, although it has been largely supplanted by radio communications.

The signal station was sited in the field above the cliffs to the northwest of the old coastguard station (in what is now 'Molly Tucker's camping field'). At 380 feet (115 metres) above sea level, it commanded a wide prospect with Start Point to the east. Sir William was taking advantage of the fact that the lighthouse at Start Point, built in 1836, was an important seamark and landfall for ships coming up-channel from the Western Approaches.

Lloyd's Signal Station, Prawle Point, 1882-1903

After 1874 Lloyds set out to bring all the private signal stations under their control and buy land to build new ones. In December 1882 they acquired a 60 year lease on an acre of land on the top of Prawle Point which included 'the old Admiralty watchhouse'. The Admiralty raised no objection, subject to Lloyds agreeing to pass on all necessary information to the Coastguard about casualties and passing vessels.

By 1883 Lloyds had installed their own signalmen and a telegraphist in the watchhouse on the Point and, as the company was in the process of taking over the *Shipping Gazette*, arranged that it should be connected with the existing station at East Prawle manned by the Coastguard. By 1888, however, the services of the Coastguards were dispensed with and the whole of the day's signalling and telegraphing was carried out at Lloyd's own station at Prawle Point.

Prawle Point C.G.F.S. (Coastguard Flagstaff), Lloyd's Signal Station and a Semaphore are all marked on this late Victorian Admiralty Chart

Up at the Lookout the duty signalman would scan the horizon for ships through his long telescope. Passing vessels wishing to be reported to Lloyds would hoist their ensign followed by their four identification flags. After identifying the signals the Lloyd's signalman would respond by hoisting the answering pennant and the telegraphist would wire the information and time of sighting to Lloyds.

LLOYD'S SIGNALLING SEMAPHORE AND MORSE	
1.Inbound ship to Lloyd's Signal Station:	2. Lloyd's Signal Station to Inbound Ship
GYKL *I am S.S. Orion*	RV *Where are you bound?*
MIK (later ZD2) *Please report me to Lloyd's*	RW *Where are you from*
Local codes:	
APIZ: *Start Point*	AETD : *Dartmouth*
AMVK: *Prawle Point*	AMPM : *Plymouth*
AOFU: *Salcombe*	AFOV: *Falmouth*

When messages could not be forwarded by telegraph, three black balls were hoisted as a triangle at the head of the signal staff to indicate that they would be forwarded as soon as possible and when the signal station was closed two black balls were hoisted horizontally. In August 1890, with the agreement of Lloyds, the Admiralty erected a semaphore mast on the Point for naval signalling.

Prawle Point was one of only five Lloyd's signal stations around the world that took night signals. Each shipping company had its own distinctive pyrotechnic display for signalling at night. The Cunard Line, for instance, displayed a blue light and two Roman candles fired in quick succession, each throwing out six blue balls to a height of about 150 feet. The answering night signal used by Lloyd's signalmen consisted of a Roman candle throwing eight balls – two red, six blue and then two white – to a height of about fifty feet.

Detail from the 1896 Admiralty Chart showing Prawle Point from the SW

SHIP-TO-SHORE SIGNALLING METHODS

1.CODE FLAG	2. SEMAPHORE	3. MORSE (by flashlight)

3. MORSE (by flashlight)

A ·—	B —···	C —·—·	D —··
E ·	F ··—·	G ——·	H ····
I ··	J ·———	K —·—	L ·—··
M ——	N —·	O ———	P ·——·
Q ——·—	R ·—·	S ···	T —
U ··—	V ···—	W ·——	X —··—
Y —·——	Z ——··		

4. PYROTECHNICS at night: (coloured flares)

In addition to publishing the shipping reports in Lloyd's List, Lloyds sold the information to local newspapers for inclusion in their Shipping News, as in this example from the 22 March 1888 edition of the Western Morning News: 'Prawle Point, Signalled bound up: *City of Dortmund*, steamer, Dublin; *Calder*, steamer, Goole; *City of Bristol*, steamer, Dublin. Signalled bound down: *Vaderland*, steamer, Antwerp; *Jane Herbert*, brigantine, Aberystwyth; *Cecil Brindley*, schooner, Aberystwyth; *S.L.Q.W.*, Italian barque; *Caroline*, schooner, Fowey'.

In 1895 John Page described the activity at Prawle Point when viewed from Bolt Head: 'Prawle Point is only three miles away, and we can distinctly see the bright string of flags streaming out of the signal station, answering other flags hoisted on that great liner driving steadily up channel. For the Prawle is an important signal station'. By 1899 the Lloyd's station was in constant use: 'One of Lloyd's signal stations is situated at Prawle Point, and passing vessels including some of the largest mail-boats, together with ships belonging to HM Navy, are constantly seen signalling on their way up or down the Channel'.

The Lloyd's signallers also reported vessels in distress. On 16 February 1889, for example, the signallers telegraphed the Customs Office at Dartmouth to report that a dismasted vessel, the barque *Chrystaline* of Liverpool, was in sight with signals of distress flying. She was later taken in tow to Dartmouth.

The New Coastguard Station at Prawle Point 1903-1913

From 1 September 1903, under an agreement between the Admiralty and Lloyds, Lloyd's signalling throughout the United Kingdom, was taken over by the Admiralty controlled Coastguard service. The Admiralty had found it difficult to provide signals training and practice at coastguard stations when the average work done with naval ships was only one word a day and so the Admiralty came up with the bright idea of undertaking commercial signalling work on behalf of Lloyds and using the income received from them to reduce the running costs of the station.

Lloyd's Signal Station and Admiralty Coastguard Lookout c1913

In 1903, with the lease of the old Coastguard station at East Prawle about to expire, the Admiralty established a new station below the Lookout at Prawle Point. The latter now became both a Lloyd's Signal Station and an Admiralty Coastguard Lookout. The new row of terraced cottages was built in 1904-5 to house the chief officer, a petty officer, eight men and their families, together with the station office at the eastern end. A communal wash-house equipped with a boiler and a manual water pump was built at the rear. Water was pumped up from three large underground tanks supplied by the run-off from the rear slope of the cottage roofs.

The coastguards and their families must have regretted the move from the village to such an isolated location. The one and half mile road from East Prawle was no more than a rough, muddy track and it was sometimes easier to have belongings delivered by boat rather than by horse and wagon. The children walked to school, often across the fields, and on their return brought back milk and bread. It was only after 1935, when the road was tarmacadamed, that the butcher and baker delivered there.

Opposite: The new Coast-guard Station at Prawle Point built in 1904-5. The chief officer's house was on the left and the station watchhouse and office on the right

Centre: The Coastguard cottages today. Most are now holiday homes

J. Wilson, the builder of the new coastguard station, apparently had enough bricks rejected by the Admiralty's clerk of works, or left over at the end of the contract, to build Maelcombe House along the coast to the east. Running out of money, Wilson subsequently sold the house to Captain Harold Helby RN, a former Inspecting Officer of Coastguards for the Salcombe division.

Wilson also got the contract to insert a telescope window up at the Prawle Point Lookout and in 1908 William Tucker installed two galvanised iron water tanks 'to remedy the inadequacy of the existing supply to the lookout house'.

Above: Maelcombe House to the east of Prawle, built with bricks left over from the new Coastguard station.

The relocation of the East Prawle station to Prawle Point in 1904 increased the distance from the next station to the east, Hallsands, to seven miles and left Lannacombe Bay with poor coverage. So a subsidiary station at Lannacombe was opened in the same year. On the other hand, because of its close proximity to the new Prawle station, the Rickham Coastguard station at Gara Rock was no longer required and so it was closed in 1909.

Coastguard Cottages at Ivy Cove, Lannacombe

The boundaries of both the Prawle Point and the Lannacombe Coastguard stations are still demarcated with stones bearing the Admiralty anchor emblem. The station at Lannacombe comprised a terrace of three coastguard

Admiralty Boundary Stones. Left: Lannacombe. Right: Prawle Point

cottages with a separate single storey watchhouse in front. Local fisherman William Login bought the station when it closed in 1922 (see page 29).

The coastguards were expected to both read and send eighteen words per minute with semaphore flags and ten with a flashing lamp. With the new acetylene fuel the range of the flashing lamp extended to twelve miles. In addition a Far Resounding Foghorn, used for Morse signalling, was supplied by the Admiralty to the coastguards at Prawle Point in 1910. When the telephone came into use in the early 1890s the Coastguard was one of the first services to recognise its advantages and, at quite an early stage, a line was stretched right round the coast. All posts and stations in a district were on the same line – an individual ring in longs and shorts being allotted to every instrument. On 4 August 1907 the duty coastguard at Prawle used the telephone to summon Salcombe lifeboat when the ketch ***Bona*** of Ipswich went ashore, at night in dense fog, on the west side of Prawle Point.

10. THE FIRST WORLD WAR

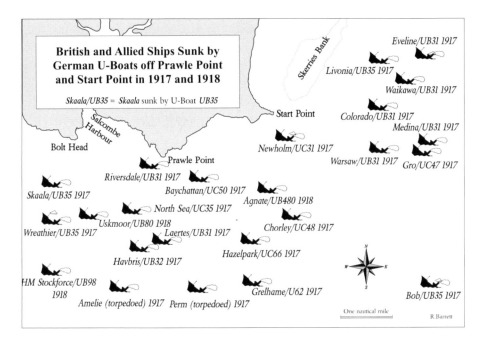

British and Allied Ships Sunk by German U-Boats off Prawle Point and Start Point in 1917 and 1918

Skaala/UB35 = Skaala sunk by U-Boat UB35

Eveline/UB31 1917
Livonia/UB35 1917
Waikawa/UB31 1917
Colorado/UB31 1917
Medina/UB31 1917
Newholm/UC31 1917
Warsaw/UB31 1917   Gro/UC47 1917
Riversdale/UB31 1917
Baychattan/UC50 1917
Skaala/UB35 1917
Agnate/UB480 1918
North Sea/UC35 1917
Uskmoor/UB80 1918
Chorley/UC48 1917
Wreathier/UB35 1917
Laertes/UB31 1917
Hazelpark/UC66 1917
Havbris/UB32 1917
HM Stockforce/UB98 1918
Grelhame/U62 1917
Bob/UB35 1917
Amelie (torpedoed) 1917   Perm (torpedoed) 1917

One nautical mile

R.Barrett

War Signal Station 1913-23

In 1913 the Prawle Point station was put on a war footing and renamed a War Signal Station. 'Signal exercise was carried out constantly in all coastguard stations, but in the War Signal Stations, it was of very much greater importance. There they carried out exercise every morning in the Morse flag, semaphore and telegraphy, and every night in the flash lamp and telegraphy. Every station officer kept a book showing the daily marks of every man, so that it is not surprising that the coastguards were very highly valued for their signalling power when war broke out.' (*F. Bowen*) Most of the stations were equipped with 500 candle-power shutter searchlights which enabled them to send Morse code over a considerable distance.

At the outset of the war in 1914, many of the Coastguard stations were closed down, whilst others were taken over by the Army (and in some cases by the Sea Scouts!). The coastguards, as naval reservists were generally drafted into old naval ships, (such as the ill-fated cruisers *Aboukir*, *Hogue* and *Crecy* – all sunk by just one U-boat soon after the outbreak of war).

However, no attempt was made to cut down on the crews of the War

Signal Stations which 'were hard at it day and night...HM ships worked through them when communicating with the Admiralty while close inshore, while they also reported and observed all movements of merchant ships. The reports that came to anxious ship-owners through the war signal stations were invaluable when the German submarines were contriving to sink scores of our ships every day' (*F. Bowen*).

Royal Naval Air Service Prawle and RAF Prawle Point 1916-18

The sea off Prawle Point was a notorious 'killing ground' for German U-boats venturing into Channel waters, with at least 25 British or allied 'merchantmen' sunk, between 1917 and 1918, within visual range of the Prawle Lookout. Two U-boat commanders, Oberleutnant Bieber of *UB31* and Oberleutnant Stoter of *UB35* were particularly active in the waters around Start and Prawle during the closing months of 1917, with Bieber accounting for eleven and Stoter four merchant steamers.

One of Bieber's victims was the 2,805 ton **Riversdale** which beached close to Prawle Point after being torpedoed. *Riversdale* was an 'armed merchant-man' carrying 4,000 tons of coal from the Tyne to Italy. On 18 December 1917, when she was a mile south of Prawle, her gunner saw a U-boat periscope and immediately fired off four shells from his 12-pounder. Bieber in *UB31*, retaliated by firing a torpedo into the *Riversdale's* port bow, flooding her forward hold. With his ship heeling badly, Captain John Simpson ran the *Riversdale* into Elender Cove where the crew abandoned her. On 28 December she was pulled off stern first by tugs but, after she had been towed about half a mile, the sea began to break over her and she sank by the bow. She now lies upright in deep water just off Prawle Point.

Anti-submarine airship patrols were flown from Mullion in Cornwall but they met with little success and high losses (in July 1916, airship *C8* crashed off Start Point killing three members of

A World War I Coastal Class Airship

the crew). On at least one occasion the airships were mistaken for enemy Zeppelins. On 28 February 1916 alarm bells were ringing at Devonport when Prawle Point War Signal Station relayed by telegraph a message from Dartmouth Coastguard reporting that Zeppelins had been seen heading

*Telegram sent on 28 February
1916 from Prawle Point War
Signal Station to C-in-C Devonport
warning of approaching Zeppelins*

towards Plymouth. It turned out to be a British airship which had failed to report its identity.

'A wireless direction-finding (DF) station was erected at Mullion and at Prawle Point and these bases took regular cross-bearings of the patrols operating in the south-western approaches, using the call-signs transmitted every hour by the airships. This enabled the position of each airship to be determined accurately.' *(P. London)* Unfortunately it is not clear whether the DF station was sited at Prawle Point or on the Prawle aerodrome described below.

In March 1917, RNAS (Royal Naval Air Service) Cattewater, the seaplane station at Mount Batten, became operational and was equipped with Short 184s. The pilot of one of these planes was later to drop a bomb on a whale off Prawle Point hitting its tail – he had mistaken it for a U-boat!

Shortly afterwards, in April 1917, **RNAS Prawle** was opened. It was the first airfield established in South-West England for land planes. It covered an extensive area of flat land west of Higher House Farm, where the fields are still known as the 'Aerodrome'. Four canvas-covered hangars housed the flight of Sopwith 1½ Strutter bi-planes. The facilities provided for the airmen were minimal – some were accommodated in huts, but most were under canvas. With Kingsbridge, the nearest town, eight miles away down narrow country lanes, the only entertainment was the village inn and the

Prawle Aerodrome – RNAS Prawle, 1917, the first airfield established in South-West England for land aeroplanes (Richard Partridge)

YMCA hut. 'The camp Padre would send out appeals to people to donate indoor games and magazines for the

179 men who were based there, and the station lived up to its name 'Lonely Prawle'.' (*G. Wasley*)

Six of the Sopwith bi-planes, in the Prawle Flight of No. 54 Squadron RNAS, were involved in accidents within three months of delivery and, within four months of the station being opened, all the serviceable aircraft were withdrawn to the Western Front.

Sopwith 1½ Strutter , RNAS Prawle

In the following year, when the RNAS and Royal Flying Corps merged in April 1918 to become the RAF, the coastal patrol scheme was re-instated and **RAF Prawle Point** re-opened as a base for DH6 and DH9 bi-planes. 'The Prawle flight of DH9s was attached to 254 Squadron and used for anti-submarine patrols, suffering mixed fortunes. In July a flight of nine Airco DH6 biplanes were sent to RAF Prawle. Within three months five were involved in accidents...*C5200* crashed at Gara Rock.' *(G.Wasley)*

DH9 of 254 Squadron RAF

DH6 of 254 Squadron RAF

After the war, the airmen's huts were acquired by locals and three were re-erected in and around the village. One became the Pig's Nose Hall, and another the Willows, an accommodation block for the market garden workers and staff at Maelcombe House on the coast.

Towards the end of the war, decoy merchant vessels known as Q ships were in operation in the waters off Prawle as a further countermeasure

Ground crew RNAS Prawle (Richard Partridge)

Lieutenant Harold Auten VC, DSC, RNR, Commander of the Q ship HMS Stock Force. Awarded the Victoria Cross after sinking UB98 off Prawle Point on 30 July 1918

against U-boats. A Q ship appeared to be an easy target, but in fact carried hidden armaments. When fired upon, a so-called 'panic party' would 'abandon' the Q Ship in order to lure the surfaced U-boat within range of its hidden guns.

At 5pm on 30 July 1918, the 360 ton Q ship, **HMS Stock Force**, commanded by Lieutenant Harold Auten DSC RNR, was five miles off Prawle Point when she was struck by a torpedo from *UB98*. The explosion wrecked the fore part of the ship, including the bridge, and wounded two officers and three ratings. The panic party immediately abandoned ship whilst the captain, the two gun crews and the engine-room staff remained at their posts, even though the ship was sinking. The submarine then came to the surface about a half a mile away, but the men in the boat successfully lured it within range of the hidden guns. Lieutenant Auten withheld fire until both of his guns could bear. Shell after shell was then poured into *UB98* until she sank by the stern.

The *Stock Force* was kept afloat by the exertions of her ship's company for several hours. She then sank with colours flying, and her crew was taken off by two torpedo boats and a trawler. The action was cited as one of the finest examples of coolness, discipline and good organisation in the history of Q ships and, two months after the action, Lieutenant Auten was awarded the Victoria Cross.

The Salcombe Lifeboat Disaster 1916

In the middle of the Great War the small community of Salcombe suffered a terrible loss when the lifeboat **William and Emma** capsized on Salcombe Bar after returning from an abortive mission near Prawle Point. Thirteen of the fifteen-man crew were drowned. At 5.12am on Friday, 27 October 1916, watchkeepers at Prawle Point sighted a distress signal off Langerstone Point. Sending a man to rouse the rest of the coastguard crew, the Chief Officer,

Leonard May, passed a message by telephone to Salcombe: 'from C.O. Prawle, to S.O. Salcombe: signal of distress on Meg Rock, Langerstone Point'. One of the coastguards was sent up to the village to call out the rocket team.

It was about 6am when the maroons were fired in Salcombe to call out the lifeboat crew. With a furious south-westerly gale blowing over the

The Salcombe Lifeboat William and Emma before her fatal capsize on Salcombe Bar on 27 October 1916. Painting by Paul Deacon

Bar, doubts were raised as to whether the boat could get through, but Coxswain Sam Distin dismissed them. Soon the boat was plunging through breaker after breaker, and then, shaking herself free, shaped a course eastward to Prawle. Shortly afterwards word reached Salcombe that the crew of the stranded vessel, the **Western Lass**, had been brought safely ashore by the rocket life-saving team.

At 7.40am Chief Officer May returned to the Prawle Point Lookout having successfully organised the rescue of the schooner's crew. From there he saw the lifeboat pass the Point. Splendidly handled, she was 'going like a greyhound'. May had no day signals to tell the crew that their services were not needed. On rounding Prawle Point the crew saw the *Western Lass*, but no sign of anyone aboard. Coming in close the cox'n spotted the rocket line across her and said 'That's it lads, let's go home'. It was a cruel beat

William and Emma Lifeboat. Model by Mike Atfield in Salcombe Maritime Museum

back. The wind had now backed southerly and was near hurricane force. When they reached the Bar they saw it was not fit to cross and twice they turned away.

On the third approach the cox'n again said 'What about it lads, shall we try it?' It was now after ten o'clock and the men had been out for over three hours. They were cold, wet and exhausted and the alternative was a long haul round to Dartmouth. So the cox'n ordered the mainsail to be lowered and the drogue put out (a hollow canvas cone towed astern to keep the boat end-on to the waves). Then, as they started lowering the jib, a huge sea struck the boat and she 'pitch-poled' end over end, flinging the men into the boiling surf. All fifteen managed to get back to the lifeboat but, not being a self-righter, all they could do was to cling to her bottom as she was dragged seawards by the ebbing tide. Two or three times they were washed off and each time fewer of them managed to scramble back. Then a bigger sea swept them all away and out of reach of the boat.

The news that the lifeboat had capsized immediately flashed through the town. Pitiful cries of distress were heard from those whose menfolk were in peril. Soon a number of men organised themselves into a life-saving party and crossed by ferry to the Portlemouth side. When they reached Limebury Point they found the wreckage of the lifeboat in a small cove and, clinging to a rock about 50 feet offshore, two of the crew.

Numerous attempts were made to throw a weighted line to them. Eventually, one of the survivors, Edwin Distin, managed to catch the rope and secured it around his fellow survivor, Bill Johnson. They were the only members of that gallant crew to be saved.

The fifteen-man crew of the ill fated lifeboat William and Emma. Only two men survived: W. Johnson and Edwin Distin

11. BETWEEN THE WARS

The War Signal Station in 1922

The photograph above shows the alterations made to the Signal Station at Prawle Point during the First World War. A raised platform, with a stone retaining wall, had been built immediately in front, to provide a base for a large signalling projector. The lattice mast nearby is a mystery. It appears to be a wireless aerial, suggesting that the station was equipped as a wireless signal station during the war. Another possibility is that this was the aerial for the airship DF station referred to on page 59. Behind the projector and aerial mast is the Admiralty mast, with an ensign flying from the yardarm.

Royal Naval Shore Signal Station, Prawle Point 1926-51

A post-war review led to the Coastguard being transferred, in 1923, from the Admiralty to the Board of Trade and 'for the first time in its history Britain had a specialised staff devoted to coast-watching and life-saving'. However, the Lloyds/Admiralty agreement was so watertight that the Admiralty was forced to continue to operate the Lloyd's Signal Stations under its control, where the 'remnants of the old force were still to be seen in their naval jumpers and bell-bottomed trousers for many years to come'. Lloyds refused to end the contract, and so it was that Prawle Point remained a naval shore establishment right up until 1951.

In May 1925, the remnant of the old Coastguard was named 'The Royal Naval Shore Signal Service' and Prawle became one of nineteen Royal

Naval Shore Signal Stations in the UK. In addition there were sixteen RN Shore Wireless Telegraphy Stations, the nearest being Portland Bill, Rame Head and the Lizard.

In 1932, the Admiralty, still keen to reduce its commitment, agreed with Lloyds that Prawle should become a day station only. However, the naval signalmen were given permission to carry out voluntary night signalling, in return for a payment of 2s 6d (12½p) for each vessel they reported.

The Signal Station c1930. The Admiralty white ensign is flying from the mast on the right. The mast flying Lloyd's blue ensign stood to the left of the man in the picture

On watch c1937. The telescope is mounted on a revolving table enabling it to be easily traversed through a 180° horizontal arc

Photographs of the Signal Station, taken in the mid 1930s, show it in operation at a time when one contemporary writer described it as 'the famous Lloyd's Signal Station'. *(R.A.J. Walling)* The photograph below shows an officer looking through a huge brass telescope, extending to 5 or 6 feet in length, mounted on a revolving table.

When the front of the lookout was re-built in 2002, the base of the old telescope platform was revealed. Also unearthed were three playing cards and a penny piece, thereby solving another mystery – how the watchkeepers passed the long winter nights!

The duty officer, telescope and mount would have filled the forward watch-room, and all the space behind would have been taken up with a small chart table/writing desk and chair, signal flag locker and other signalling equip-

ment, manuals and logbooks and, of course a stove and kettle. Lime was brought up for the 'bucket and chuck-it' toilet and coal for fuel. The top-hung telescope windows were left open in all but the worst weather, so it would often have been cold, in spite of the stove.

Prawle Point 'Ship Trap' 1918 -1939

Over the years, Prawle Point has built up an unenviable reputation as a magnet for stricken vessels and Peter Mitchell, author of the '*Wrecker's Guide to South-West Devon*', refers to the Point's outstanding ability to act as a 'ship trap'. 'Whilst many ships have struck the outside of Prawle Point, a significant number have managed to end up caught in between the jaws of the island and the mainland's shore, and that's where the real ship trap lies.'

Many of the ships driven onto the west side of the Point had been bound up-channel in thick or foggy weather. Their masters, unable to fix their position by taking sightings, would have had to fall back on dead reckoning to shape their vessel's course. Too many, it would seem, made insufficient allowance in their calculations for leeway, or for the tidal set between Eddystone and Prawle. Even on the ebb, this can tend to draw ships towards the shore and those unfortunate enough to be driven towards Prawle's projecting headland would often be sucked by local eddies into the 'ship trap', like fish in a net.

One ship caught in the trap was the 880 ton Dutch coaster, **Betsy Anna.** On 17 August 1926 she became stranded in thick fog between the Point and the Island. When the tide went out, the crew walked ashore. She was towed off on 3 October and taken into Salcombe for temporary repairs. Her luck, however, finally ran out nine days later, when she sank after her tow parted whilst rounding Portland Bill.

Dense fog also contributed to the wreck of the **Ida,** of Antwerp, which entered the 'ship trap' on 22 September 1930. The *Ida* was on passage, with a crew of twelve, from Cardiff to Portsmouth with 580 tons of coal. Safely weathering Bolt Head, she failed to clear Prawle Point. The duty officer up at the Lookout saw her flares and immediately called for lifeboat assistance. Both the Plymouth and Torbay lifeboats responded (there being no lifeboat in Salcombe between 1925 and 1930). The Prawle life-saving apparatus was also summoned and soon afterwards the rocket line was successfully directed over the vessel. One man had already swum ashore but the remaining eleven were hoisted up the 150 foot cliff in the breeches buoy. It was hoped to re-float her, but she later broke in two and the aft section sank in deep water.

Betsy Anna 1926

Benmohr 1931

Ida 1930

Louise Yvonne 1935

Prawle Point 'Ship Trap' Victims 1926-35

Prawle Life Saving Appliance Company circa 1930.
Station Officer Fred Gordon is in the middle of the front row

At 5pm on 25 February 1931, both the Salcombe lifeboat and the Prawle Rocket team were summoned by the Prawle Point watch officer when the 5,920 ton steamship, **Benmohr**, on passage from Avonmouth to her home port of Leith, ran ashore in rough seas at the Point, practically on top of the wreck of the *Ida*. The captain, hoping to re-float her, asked the lifeboat to stand by. The rocket team meanwhile rigged a breeches buoy while the captain waited for tugs to arrive. With no sign of them that evening, the rocket crew maintained their cliff-top vigil throughout the night. When the weather worsened during the following afternoon, the captain relented and the apparatus was used to bring off 43 of the crew of 49. It was a textbook operation, apparently taking only fifty minutes to complete. *Benmohr* remained on the rocks for a fortnight before she was refloated by the salvage vessel *Restorer* and a German tug *Eros*. Eleven years later, in March 1942, she was sunk by a German U-Boat off the West African coast.

The 'ship trap' claimed another victim at 3am on 27 August 1935, when, again in thick fog, the French motor vessel **Louise Yvonne** ran in between the Point and the Island. She was on her way from Penzance to Torquay with a cargo of onions and had a crew of four and the captain's two daughters aboard. They all managed to scramble ashore, and stayed in the village for a week, hoping to salvage both ship and cargo. However, the onions became contaminated with fuel oil and the vessel was a total wreck. Her bows are still visible at low spring tide, in spite of the fact that the coaster *Heye-P* piled on top of her in 1979.

Wrecks at Lannacombe and Rickham 1927 and 1934

Dense fog and faulty navigation played their part in the stranding of the 100 ton steamer ***Branksea*** on the night of 1 September 1927, when she struck the rocks between Lannacombe Cove and Mattiscombe Sand. She was carrying china clay from Par to the Dutch port of Terneuzen. A London holidaymaker, camping on shore, heard the steamer's siren signals before

she struck so, grabbing a bugle, he rushed to the beach and played 'Come to the cookhouse door boys' – the first tune that came into his head, to warn the crew that land was near. A few minutes later, the steamer signalled in Morse, 'We are ashore'.

The steamer Branksea on the rocks at Lannacombe, 1 September 1927

Lannacombe fishermen came to the scene and later the Torbay lifeboat stood by, but the crew eventually came off in their own boats. The steamer was re-floated on a following high tide.

On 11 April 1934, the French trawler, 150 ton ***Touquet***, from Boulogne, with a twenty-man crew, was stranded for about twelve hours on the rocks between Moor Sand and Gara Rock, after running into a bank of dense fog.

The French trawler Touquet ashore east of Gara Rock, 11 April 1934

The captain first tried to get off by reversing the engines at full speed but, that having failed, he sent a wireless S.O.S. and called for a tug. The captain declined the help of the Salcombe lifeboat and, with the help of the tug, refloated his ship next day.

Gara Rock Guest House and Hotel

Back in 1909, the Coastguard Station at Rickham had been sold by auction at Kingsbridge to the Jordan family of Plymouth, who then converted it to a family guest house. The accommodation was rather primitive in the early days with no bathrooms and an outside lavatory. However, after the First World War the family embarked on an extensive improvement programme. In 1919, a second storey was added, and by 1936 the Gara Rock Guest House was able to claim 'perfect sanitation, separate tables, central heating, and private flats with bathrooms'.

Gara Rock Hotel before the Second World War

In the years before the Second World War, the hotel had built up a prestigious reputation and was attracting celebrities such as Sir Laurence Olivier, Margaret Rutherford, and the Poet Laureate Sir John Betjeman. One of the many attractions for the guests was a nine-hole golf course laid out on Rickham Common to the west.

In 1940 the hotel was requisitioned as accommodation for officers at RAF West Prawle. When the property was handed back five years later, it was purchased by Commander Lloyd Owen, who re-opened it as a family hotel in 1946. For a number of years guests had to bring their ration books and their own soap and towels and the rooms were furnished with ex-service NAAFI style furniture. Just as the hotel was recovering from post-war restrictions, disaster struck in 1950 when the staff accommodation block was partially destroyed by fire. In 1961 Commander Owen was forced to retire through ill-health and the hotel was sold to the Richards family from Kent. In 1971 the old coastguard lookout was re-thatched and, for one season only, was opened as a licensed bar, making it the smallest 'pub' in Britain.

In 2004, Gara Rock Hotel was purchased by the Coast Group, who closed it in 2006 and commenced the redevelopment of the site for luxury apartments and cottages in 2008.

12. THE SECOND WORLD WAR

Enjoying a summer's evening in the 1930s. Note the large signalling projector

All present and correct. The crew of the Royal Naval Shore Signal Station just before the outbreak of war

Guarding the Coast during World War II

With war looming in 1939 the Royal Naval Shore Signal Stations were put on constant watch. Like the Coastguard stations they were required 'to report any warship, British or foreign, and any other ship not usually seen in the area, which was acting suspiciously'.

In July 1940 the Prawle Point Lookout was camouflaged as a war measure. Also in that year the Admiralty built an engine house to the east of the Lookout (the present Visitor Centre), to house a generator for powering the signalling projector. This replaced an earlier acetylene generator installed in 1927 in a smaller building. The Admiralty's Naval Reserve Office was at pains to point out that, for blackout reasons, the generator was not to be used for lighting the Lookout.

In addition to the Lookout at Prawle, Coast Watching Posts were set up at the Gara Rock Hotel to the west and, to the east, at Lannacombe coastguard lookout and at Great Mattiscombe, where an observation hut was sited above the beach. These posts were manned day and night by Auxiliary Coastguards who formed part of the Intelligence Section of the Coast Life Saving Corps. At the start of the war, the Gara Rock detachment comprised seven men led by Fred Jordan of the hotel but, when the hotel was requisitioned in 1940, watchkeeping was undertaken by RAF personnel. At Lannacombe, Frank Login led a team which included his three brothers, whilst at Mattiscombe, William Cole, the farmer at Start Farm, led a team of ten men from Hallsands, Bickerton and Kellaton. The residents of Maelcombe House also signed up for coastwatching duties.

On 9 July 1940, the watchkeepers at Prawle Point and the Coast Watching Posts would have witnessed the sinking of the 534 ton Latvian steamer ***Talvaldis*** after she was bombed and machine-gunned by a German aircraft off the Point. A motor boat from Lannacombe Bay rescued six of the crew from a raft and the Salcombe lifeboat rescued another six in a waterlogged boat.

Off the coast, German E-boats were a constant menace, 'moving into quiet bays such as Gara Rock, during darkness, to anchor up and wait for signs of allied ships to pass and then attack them from the unexpected shore side and so shore patrols, which included Home Guardsmen, were set up to try and spot them' *(P.A.F. Pearce).* An Admiralty trawler, the 596 ton **HMS Jasper**, was torpedoed by an E-boat, on 1 December 1942, one and a half miles SSW of Prawle Point. Two days later **HMS Penlyan**, a 1050 ton Hunt Type 111 destroyer, was sunk midway between Prawle and the Start, by a torpedo from E-boat *S115*, whilst escorting a coastal convoy. Two officers and 34 ratings were lost – five officers and 112 ratings rescued. Later in the war, ***James Otis,*** an American Liberty Ship with 76 men aboard, went ashore in Lannacombe Bay on 7 February 1945. The Salcombe lifeboat stood by until Plymouth tugs refloated her.

In addition to E-boats, the watchkeepers at Prawle Point were on constant

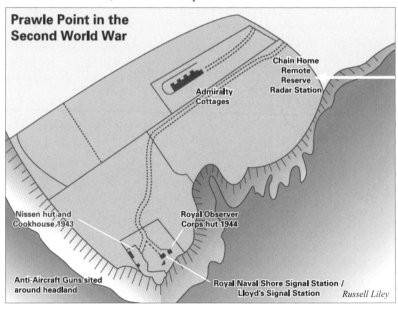

Prawle Point in the Second World War

Chain Home Remote Reserve Radar Station

Admiralty Cottages

Nissen hut and Cookhouse 1943

Royal Observer Corps hut 1944

Anti-Aircraft Guns sited around headland

Royal Naval Shore Signal Station / Lloyd's Signal Station

Russell Liley

lookout for German aircraft. A raid by a German Dornier bomber, which took place in June 1940, blasted two huge craters close to two cottages at Stoneybridge, Rickham. It is possible that the bomber's target was the Radar Station at nearby RAF West Prawle. Three months later, in September 1940, Rickham farm workers were gathering in the harvest when a flight of aircraft suddenly came roaring out of the fog and landed in their midst. Although the planes had RAF markings, the workers were suspicious of the 'foreign-sounding' pilots dressed in strange uniforms. So, with pitchforks at the ready, they escorted them to Rickham Farm where it was soon established that the airmen were Polish and based at RAF Exeter. They had been scrambled to intercept German planes returning from a bombing raid on Plymouth. Flying beyond their safe range, the Poles were obliged to make forced landings in the stubble fields.

On 15 March 1942, two Spitfire VB fighters belonging to the Polish 317 squadron, encountered thick fog when returning to RAF Bolt Head from a sweep over northern France and crashed landed near Prawle, one towards Rickham and the other in Higher Shallowpool field, south of the old coast-guard cottages at East Prawle.

In 1943 a Nissen hut was erected by the War Office just to the west of the Prawle Point Lookout. Anti-aircraft guns were mounted on the Point, and so the buildings presumably provided accommodation for the duty gunners. More personnel were drafted here in July 1944, when the Air Ministry set up a Royal Observer Corps hut near the Lookout.

Nancy Budd, née Nash, moved to No. 6, Coastguard Cottages at Prawle Point in 1941. Her father worked up at the 'watch-box' and she clearly remembers the rough times when the gale cone was hoisted and the sea spray would lash the bedroom window. Margaret Doust also lived in the cottages as a young girl and remembers her mother taking supper and a hot drink up to the Lookout when grandfather (Albert Morgan) was on late watch. 'Pleasures were simple and food grown in the front garden was fresh and varied. On Sunday nights after church at the little Methodist Chapel we would often sing hymns together.'

It would have been a night to remember for the officers on duty up at the Prawle Point 'watch-box', on the evening of 4 June 1944, when they observed part of the D-Day invasion fleet sailing out of Salcombe Harbour. The 66 ships and the many auxiliary vessels were part of the American amphibious 'Force U' which landed at Utah Beach, Normandy.

RAF West Prawle 1939-57

With war threatening in the summer of 1939, RAF West Prawle was set up, as part of the Chain Home System, to provide RDF (Radar) cover for the approaches to Exeter and Plymouth. In 1940 the RAF requisitioned the hotel at Gara Rock as a headquarters and mess for RAF and WRAF officers. The RAF remained there for three years and was followed by the Royal Navy.

As the West Prawle site developed, the personnel were accommodated either on the site itself, beyond Moor Farm, or in a camp, known as the B site, set up at the north end of East Prawle village off Town Road. At its peak as many as 700 service personnel were based around Prawle. These included Royal Artillery gunners and RAF Regiment personnel defending the radar site. 'The radar at West Prawle was the AMES Type1 West Coast type with two 365 foot guyed masts supporting the Transmitter curtain aerial. There were two transmitters each with their own aerial system. The Transmitter site was located beyond the lane down to the farm, north of the Portlemouth road. The receiver aerials were 200 foot wooden towers located near the ops. block/receiver stations. The site was surrounded by ten foot high steel fencing topped with barbed wire.' *(Ron Bates)*

In 1942 the RAF set up another Radar Station above Start Point as part of the Chain Home (Low) system. This was taken over by the Americans in 1943 who re-equipped it with Microwave Early Warning Radar.

Back at West Prawle there was also a **GEE station** which enabled aircraft crews to calculate their position with reasonable accuracy. GEE was the most widely used radio-navigational aid of the war and the forerunner of Loran and Decca radio 'navaid' systems. In addition GEE-H and Oboe precision blind bombing systems greatly increased the accuracy of aircraft on bombing raids. The secrecy surrounding GEE and Oboe ground stations exceeded even the high level accorded to normal radar, and personnel were not usually allowed to leave the site during their posting.

The Chain Home Station at West Prawle was backed up by a **Remote Reserve Site** on the coast near the Prawle Point Coastguard Cottages where the substantial remains of three bunkers can still be seen. According to P.G. Hope, a radar engineer at West Prawle during the war, 'There came a time when the radar beams from the main West Prawle transmitters were rumbled. The Messerschmitts etc., learnt to fly under them. This led to the hasty construction of a smaller unit down on Prawle beach'. The bunker

*Receiver Block below the Coastguard
Cottages*

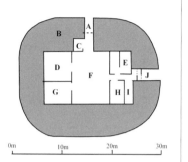

Plan of Type C Receiver Block
A: goods entrance, B: earth revetment,
C: transformer room, D: air conditioning
plant, E: radio room, F: receiver room,
G: apparatus room H: PBX,
I: battery room, J: personnel entrance

Transmitter Block in foreground

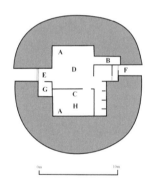

Plan of Type C Transmitter Block
A: roof vent, B: bay for feed-throughs,
C: cable duct,   D: transmitter equipment
E: goods entrance, F: personnel entrance.
G: transformer room, H: ventilator system

*Generator Block with concrete walls
exposed at the top of the earth bank*

*Source: Len Thomas, Subterranea
Britannica website*

Prawle Point Remote Reserve Radar Station

nearest the sea was the receiver building, the small mound to the east the transmitter block. A third, large bunker (with its thick blast proof concrete walls now largely exposed) was the generator block. Two large generators were housed here, powered by diesel oil stored in large tanks. Two wooden masts, about 300 feet high, stood on the site.

The receiver block housed equipment which presented a display to the WAAF operator, on a CRT (cathode ray tube). P.G. Hope recalls that 'an experienced Station Officer, and most of those under her, could identify most aircraft, shipping, and the occasional shoals of porpoises. German aircraft could be spotted taking off from airfields in northern France, allowing precious minutes to get our own fighters airborne'. At least half a dozen Nissen huts were dotted about the site, and all the buildings were covered by camouflage netting supported on wire stays. At a later stage in the war it is believed that American servicemen operated the radar here.

The Remote Reserve site was heavily defended. Wire fencing was placed around the perimeter, with a guardhouse near the bottom of the lane. Machine gun posts were set up above Copstone Cove, on Signalhouse Point and on Prawle Point itself. Further to the east, there was a 20mm gun emplacement at the top of Sharper's Head. Anti-aircraft Bofor guns, firing 40mm shells, were placed further inland to protect the radar sites, one at Woodcombe on the left of the road coming into East Prawle. Another was sited on the old WWI aerodrome, south of the Portlemouth road where there was a Royal Artillery camp complete with ammunition dump, four or five Nissen huts, cookhouse and ablution blocks. A further anti-aircraft gun was sited to the west at High House Farm.

RAF West Prawle remained operational until 1957 and, during the early years of the Cold War, was one of the most powerful radar-warning stations in the South-West, with over 200 RAF personnel based there. The domestic camp at East Prawle, off Town Road, known as the 'Garden Camp' because of its trim gardens and model husbandry, comprised airmen's quarters, cookhouse, canteen, ablution blocks, stores and motor transport workshop, as well as a cinema, also used as a dance-hall, and a large sick-bay. The site was cleared in 1962.

Today it is difficult to conceive that this now peaceful area was alive with military activity fifty or so years ago. Only the radio masts, a few Nissen huts, bunkers, and blockhouses used as farm buildings, remain.

13. PRAWLE COASTGUARD STATION 1951-94

Lloyd's Signal Station, Prawle Point 1951-6

With the expiry of the Lloyds/ Admiralty Agreement in 1951, the Admiralty was finally free to hand over control of the station at Prawle Point to the Coastguard service. Lloyds continued to maintain an interest in Prawle, and so a fresh arrangement was negotiated whereby the Coastguards would carry out signalling at the pre-war rate of 2s 6d for each report (12½p). Lloyd's signalling at Prawle finally ceased on Sunday, 30 September 1956.

Code flag signalling at the Lizard Lloyd's Signal Station, Cornwall

HM Coastguard, Prawle Point 1951-94

In 1966 the two regular coastguards and a team of auxiliaries were maintaining a constant night watch as well as bad weather watches during the day. Night watches were of six hours' duration and were usually kept by a single officer. The equipment consisted of a telescope and telephone. Electric light, supplied from accumulators, had been installed in January 1955.

The Rocket Post in Sharper's Field, East Prawle

The East Prawle Rocket Team formed in 1878 was still going strong. By this time the apparatus was housed in the 'shed' on the village green. Sunday morning training sessions involved the whole village, and provided something of a spectacle for visitors in the holiday season. The rocket post, which still stands today in Sharper's field above Sharper's Head, was used to simulate a ship's mast.

On the morning of 31 October 1972 the Team was called out by maroons to attend the 590 ton coaster *Friars Craig* that had come ashore in thick fog east of Lannacombe Cove. Her crew had sent out a Mayday message, but it was a phone call from Mrs. Login of Ivy Cove, Lannacombe, reporting a big ship on the shore, that first alerted the Prawle coastguards. The Mayday did, however, alert the

Rocket drill practice on the 'Aerodrome' in 1960

The team in action in 1972 rescuing the crew of the Friars Craig

Winners of the Webber Cup 1963

Rocket Drill Practice on Sharper's Field 1970

Winners of the Brixham Area Cup 1970

East Prawle LSA Company
(Photos: Richard Partridge)

The Friars Craig on the rocks near Lannacombe on 31 October 1972. Four crew, including the female cook, were brought safely ashore by breeches buoy

Salcombe lifeboat, several fishing vessels and the minesweeper *HMS Kedleston.* They all converged on the area but contact was made difficult by the heavy swell.

However, the Prawle team managed to get a line across her and four of the crew were safely brought ashore. Two fishing boats towed the *Friars Craig* off and she later entered Dartmouth under her own power.

One of the duties of the coastguards at Prawle Point was to send weather reports, every three hours during a watch, to Mount Batten at Plymouth. The results were passed on to the Meteorological Office at Bracknell as input to the national forecast. Daily measurements of the hours of sunlight were also made using a sunshine recorder. This was mounted on the brick plinth which still stands in front of the Lookout. (Though a much better story is that this is the chimney of the house where the troglodytes live in the cliffs below!)

The 1970s saw the introduction of mains electricity and a VHF radio in the Lookout but, as its range was limited and few of the smaller craft had radios, it was not often used. A constant 24 hour watch, with two coastguard officers

HM Coastguard Lookout, Prawle Point in 1978. Note the overhead electricity lines

on duty, was maintained. In the mid 1970s the Start Cliff Rescue Team was formed. The six-man team included two of the lighthouse keepers at Start Point and local auxiliaries such as the Ansell brothers of Start Farm and the Foss brothers of Down Farm.

During the 1970s the coastguard service underwent major changes in response to the development of radio and electronic aids and the need to secure improved co-ordination of rescue services. Maritime Rescue Centres were set up in key locations such as Falmouth, Brixham and Portland with the emphasis on maintaining a listening, rather than a visual watch. In September 1978, in response to these changes, manning at Prawle was reduced to continuous night watches, with 'casualty risk watches' during the day, usually when wind speeds exceeded force five.

At 5am on 12 March 1978, Prawle Coastguards received a Mayday call from the 40 ton Brixham trawler **Yvette**, which had struck the rocks east of Langerstone Point, and called out the Salcombe lifeboat and the East Prawle Rocket Team. The crew, other than the owner skipper, Mike Thomas, were all brought off by breeches buoy.

They were to be the last men to be saved by means of the Prawle rocket apparatus and breeches buoy. Helicopters were already beginning to replace shore-based rocket teams as the primary means of getting the crew off a stranded ship, and the *Yvette* marked this transition by having its skipper taken off by a helicopter from the frigate *HMS Charybdis*.

In spite of all attempts to salvage her, the *Yvette* became a total wreck but, with the help of Roger Tucker of Higher House Farm and his farm workers, a great deal of her equipment was saved. Parts of the wreck can still be seen at low tide on the rocks below Sharper's Head.

Around midnight on 16 December 1979 the 296 ton German coaster **Heye-P**, loaded

Top: The Brixham trawler Yvette stranded on the rocks below Sharper's Head in March 1978. Bottom: Parts of the wreck can still be seen at low tide

The 296 ton coaster Heye-P on the rocks below Prawle Point in December 1979. The crew were winched off by a Sea King helicopter from RNAS Culdrose

with china clay, was overwhelmed by gale force nine, SW winds as she was making her way up-channel from Par, in Cornwall. Huge waves pushed her relentlessly towards the rocks below the Prawle Point Lookout. The watch-keeper saw the lights of a ship coming head-on to the rocks and fired maroons to warn of the danger. It was not long before the Salcombe lifeboat arrived on the scene but the size of the waves and the off-lying rocks prevented her from rescuing the three-man crew. When the East Prawle Rocket Team arrived, lines were fired across the *Heye-P,* but her crew made

it clear by hand signals that they would only come off by helicopter. When a *Sea King* from RNAS Culdrose arrived, a massive sea broke over the ship. Enveloped in huge sheets of spray the pilot was clearly unhappy but, with both the Prawle Team and the Start Point Cliff Team directing the light of portable search-lights onto the stricken ship, he was able to hover while the men were

The remains of Prawle Point 'Ship Trap' victims visible at low tide

quickly winched off. Apparently the transfer was so rapid that 'the last man off must have left his boots behind'! It was the last occasion that the rocket lines were fired. The remains of the *Heye-P* can still be seen, on a low spring tide, in the channel between Prawle Point and the Island, close to the bow section of the *Louis Yvonne* which sank in 1935.

In 1982 routine visual watches were stopped at Prawle Point and in 1983 a new Coastguard station was opened in East Prawle village as a base for the Prawle Point Coastguard Rescue Company. Between 1982 and 1994, the Lookout continued to be used intermittently for 'foul weather watches'. It was also manned when the Salcombe lifeboat was launched and when an event involving large numbers of boats was expected in the area. From time to time it was put to less conventional use. On one occasion, the modern day preventive service – HM Customs and the Regional Crime Squad – used it as a temporary base when mounting an operation to catch a gang of smugglers off the coast. This resulted in considerable seizures of cannabis.

Prawle Point Station Officer Jack Appleton and Brian Hodson in 1978 outside the station office

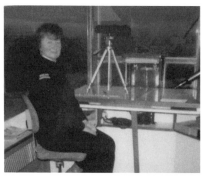

Norah Kingston on six-hour solo night watch up at the Lookout in 1981

Auxiliary Coastguards Norah Kingston and Josephine Trinick on duty in 1983 in the watchhouse

Frank Smith , awarded the RNLI Bronze Medal in 1992

On 8 January 1992 Brixham Coastguard received a distress call from the 1,159 ton coaster ***Janet C*** which had lost power in a force 8 gale, perilously close to the rocks at Start Point. A rescue helicopter was scrambled and the Salcombe lifeboat, *Baltic Exchange II,* launched. The lifeboat reached the scene first. With little hesitation, Coxswain/Mechanic Frank Smith took her in between the rocks and, in mountainous seas with the lifeboat rising and falling 35 feet, managed to get a tow line across the casualty. The first tow parted but a second was secured and the *Janet C* was towed clear. The lifeboat held the vessel in tow for three hours in violent seas until a tug was able to come up and take over. Frank Smith was later awarded the RNLI Bronze Medal for his skill and bravery.

On 18 December 1992, the largest ship to be wrecked at Prawle Point, the 9,700 ton cargo ship ***Demetrios***, came ashore in a force 10 gale. Fortunately there was no-one on board, for the *Demetrios*, formerly the

The 9,700 ton cargo ship Demetrios broken in two on the west side of Prawle Point 18 December 1992, after breaking away from a tug in a force 10 gale. She was being towed from Dunkirk to a breaker's yard in Turkey

Chinese owned *Longlin*, was being towed by a Russian tug, from Dunkirk and bound for a breaker's yard in Turkey, when the tow parted at the height of the gale. The unmanned ship drifted for over 30 miles before striking the Island, off Prawle Point, at 9.52 am. Later that day she came ashore and broke her back.

Demetrios below the Prawle Point Lookout

In scenes reminiscent of the *Gossamer* wreck 124 years previously, hundreds of people from miles around descended on the wreck, and the local police had a busy time controlling not only the traffic, but the minority of people who were intent on looting whatever they could carry away.

A local salvage company later cut up the ship and towed the scrap to Plymouth. However, the cost of the operation was to force the company into liquidation. Not all of the wreck was removed and several sections are still visible today.

The Demetrios was broken up for scrap which was then towed by barge to Plymouth

Occupation of the Prawle Point Lookout by HM Coastguard finally came to an end in 1994, when the lease was surrendered.

Parts of the Demetrios are still visible below Prawle Point

14. SAFEGUARDING THE COAST TODAY

HM Coastguard, now part of the Maritime and Coastguard Agency (MCA), remains responsible for preventing the loss of life at sea and along the coast. It is assisted locally by the volunteers who make up the Prawle Point Coastguard Rescue Team, the Salcombe Lifeboat crew and the watch-keeping team at the National Coastwatch Institution Lookout at Prawle Point.

Prawle Point Coastguard Rescue Team Station, East Prawle village

The Coastguard Rescue Team exercising below Prawle Point

Prawle Point Coastguard Rescue Team

HM Coastguard station in Town Road, which opened in 1983, is the base for the volunteer members of the Prawle Point Coastguard Rescue Team. The Team was created as a result of the amalgamation of the original Prawle Point lookout team, the East Prawle Rocket Line Team and the Start Point cliff rescue team and is responsible for the area from Slapton Line to Kingsbridge with all the coastline and estuary between. In addition to cliff rescues, the team is called upon, from time to time, to search for missing persons, including children, swimmers, and overdue walkers and, on occasions, animals. Well-rehearsed search techniques enable a large area of ground to be covered in a fairly short period of time.

RNLI Salcombe Lifeboats

Since 1869, when the first lifeboat station was established at South Sands, Salcombe's volunteer lifeboat crews have saved hundreds of lives and been involved in countless dangerous and dramatic rescues. When she is not 'out on a shout' the Tamar class, All Weather Lifeboat, *Baltic Exchange III*, lies afloat alongside her purpose-built pontoon at Salcombe. She is complemented by the *Joan Bate,* an Atlantic 75 Inshore Lifeboat, housed in a boat-house adjacent to the Lifeboat Station. Together they are called out about fifty times a year.

Salcombe All Weather and Inshore Lifeboats. (RNLI)

National Coastwatch Institution, Prawle Point

In the same year that Prawle Point Lookout closed, 1994, two fishermen drowned within sight of the former Bass Point Lookout on the Lizard Peninsula in Cornwall. This tragedy led to the formation of the National Coastwatch Institution (NCI), by concerned seafarers who saw the need to reinstate a visual watch at Bass Point and at other locations on our coasts where Coastguard lookouts had been closed. Since then NCI has expanded rapidly and now has around fifty operational stations keeping visual watch along the coastline of England and Wales. NCI watchkeepers keep a sharp

The Lookout today with the Visitor Centre on the right. The station is manned during most daylight hours after 9am

'Eyes along the Coast'.
NCI volunteers maintain the watch
365 days a year

lookout for vulnerable craft and people, such as open boats, yachts, fishing vessels, divers, walkers and sea anglers. Their aim is to minimise the time it takes to get help to anyone in trouble by passing up-to-date information to HM Coastguard who co-ordinate search and rescue. Stations are equipped with VHF radio to monitor emergency channels, telescopes, telephones, radar, and up-to-date charts. The watch-keepers, male and female, come from all walks of life and are fully trained to meet the high standards required by the NCI and the Maritime Coastguard Agency.

Prawle Point NCI station opened on 5 April 1998, when watchkeeping resumed at the old Coastguard Lookout after a lapse of four years. During that time the familiar landmark on the Point had become semi-derelict and open to the elements. It had a leaking roof, broken doors and windows and there was no water, sewerage, electricity or equipment. However, with the help of generous funding from local people, companies and bodies it was transformed into a well-equipped and efficient working station.

A local man, Captain Chris Trinick, had been instrumental in setting up a volunteer force and work began soon after the lease had been agreed with the landowners, the National Trust, in 1997. Further substantial improvements

The derelict Lookout before
restoration in 1997

Back in service: the Lookout after
its restoration by local volunteers

Major re-building works to improve the field of view from the Lookout were carried out in 2001 with the aid of generous donations

were made to the Lookout in 2001 when, with the aid of generous donations, the building was extended to the westward to improve the view over Salcombe Bar.

Since then the Prawle Point NCI Station has grown in strength and now has a fully trained team of 60 or so volunteers who turn out in all conditions to keep the station open 365 days a year. Watchkeepers maintain a watch over the waters between Start Point and Bolt Head and beyond, logging all identifiable craft passing the station. All incidents are immediately reported to HM Coastguard. The watchkeepers also monitor VHF radio channels for

Spot   *Plot*   *and Report*

Watchkeepers keep a sharp lookout for vulnerable craft and people and immediately report those that get into difficulty to HM Coastguard who, in turn, task Search and Rescue services such as Salcombe Lifeboat

Salcombe Lifeboat, Baltic Exchange III, passing Start Point Lighthouse. NCI watchkeepers work closely with the lifeboat crews, sometimes guiding them directly to a casualty by radio (RNLI)

distress and urgency calls and record weather conditions for the benefit of local seafarers.

The watchkeepers at the NCI Prawle Point Station regularly report incidents to the Coastguard involving, for instance, missing divers, dismasted yachts, engine breakdowns, upturned dinghies and injured walkers. In their role as '*Eyes along the Coast*', they make a valuable contribution to the safety of the people and craft that venture along the South Hams coast.

The station is responsible for raising its own funds to provide equipment, maintain the buildings and train its watchkeepers. NCI receives no government funding and, to maintain the watch, the station relies on the generosity of the public and the fund-raising efforts of an active and much-valued local support group, *Friends of Prawle Point*.

In 2010, the Visitor Centre, in the old World War II generator building next to the Lookout, was completely refurbished with the help of a generous grant from the Heritage Lottery Fund and is now a popular attraction for walkers on the coastal path. The Centre is open to visitors, free of charge, everyday during Lookout opening hours

National Coastwatch Stations around the English and Welsh Coasts

Protecting the Coastal Heritage

The beauty and splendour of the coastline between Start Point and Salcombe Bar, as well as its importance in terms of wildlife and geology, is reflected in the protection that it has gained over the years. It forms part of the South Devon Area of Outstanding Natural Beauty (AONB) created in 1959 and, in 1976, this section of foreshore, cliffs and raised beaches was designated a Site of Special Scientific Interest (SSSI) because of its geological and wildlife interest.

More recently the marine habitats and species on the adjacent seabed have received statutory protection through the designation, in 2011, of the Prawle Point to Plymouth Sound and Eddystone Special Area of Conservation – a Marine Conservation Zone which is soon to be extended to include the reefs between Prawle Point and Start Point.

Also offshore, both the Bronze Age and the seventeenth century Gold sites off Moor Sands are fully protected as Historic Wrecks under the Protection of Wrecks Act 1973.

Much of the coast is under the protection of the National Trust which ensures that it is managed in a sympathetic and sustainable manner. Nearly all the coastal strip between Millbay in Salcombe Harbour and Prawle Point was acquired by the Trust between 1928 and 1985. Covenants are also held over a small area in Lannacombe Bay. The Prawle Point headland was given to the Trust in 1966 by the Triangle Trust 1949 Fund and, at the same time, adjoining land was bought using locally raised Enterprise Neptune funds.

Privately owned land is in the hands of caring farmers and landowners, such as the Blackpool and Start Estate, and much of it is farmed in the interests of conservation and amenity under the Countryside Stewardship Scheme. Habitats are managed to protect wildlife such as the rare Cirl Bunting.

Running along the entire length of the coast is the South West Coast Path, a National Trail completed in the 1970s. The section between Start Point and Salcombe Bar is a popular route for both long distance walkers and those who benefit from the many fine circular walks that have been waymarked by the National Trust and the South Devon AONB Countryside Team. Details of these walks and the wildlife that can be spotted along them can be seen on the South Devon AONB website at www.southdevonaonb.org.uk

There is much of interest to see. The headlands at Start, Peartree and Prawle Points are beacons for migrating birds in spring and autumn and rare species often make a landfall here. The headlands are also excellent locations for spotting sea mammals such as dolphins, porpoises and grey seals, as well as sea birds such as gannets and cormorants. Many varieties of wild flowers, some rare, bloom throughout spring, summer and autumn and add to the wildlife interest, whilst the important geological formations are a particular attraction for field study groups.

The NCI watchkeepers at Prawle Point play a small, but important part in protecting this valuable coastal heritage by notifying the appropriate bodies of pollution and environmental damage, dangers to livestock, sightings of dolphins, porpoises and whales, harassment of wildlife and illegal diving on the historic wreck sites.

In the past people have sought to defend this coast against hostile forces. Today, in more settled times, the focus is on protecting the safety of those who venture along its shores and on safeguarding its many qualities for the benefit of generations to come.

Select Bibliography and Sources

Chapter 1. Introduction

Mottershead, Derek. *Classic Landforms of the South Devon Coast,* Geographical Association, Sheffield, 1997

Chapter 2. Early History

Born, Anne. *The History of Kingsbridge and Salcombe*, Orchard Publications, Chudleigh, 2002

Chivelstone Parish Council. *Chivelstone Millennium Book*, 2001

Elliot, Colin. *Discovering Armada Britain,* David & Charles, Newton Abbot, 1987

Exeter Archaeology. *Chivelstone Heritage Appraisal,* South Hams District Council, Totnes, 2007

Hanson, Neil. *The Confident Hope of a Miracle, the True Story of the Spanish Armada,* Corgi Books, London, 2003

Hoskins, W.G. *Devon*, Collins, London, 1954

James, Jeanne. *The Medieval Chapel at Prawle, Devon & Cornwall Notes and Queries*, Vol XL. Part V, 2009

Roberts, W.A. *Elizabethan Court Rolls of Stokenham Manor 1560-1602,* W.A. Roberts, Beeson, 1984

Russell, Percy. *Fire Beacons in Devon,* Transactions of the Devonshire Assoc., 1955

Waterhouse, Robert. *Stokenham Heritage Appraisal and East Portlemouth Heritage Appraisal,* South Hams District Council, Totnes, 2002

Chapter 3. Wrecks, Wreckers and Smugglers

Barrett, Roger. *Start Point and Its Lighthouse,* Orchard Publications, Chudleigh, 2006

Waugh, Mary. *Smuggling in Devon & Cornwall 1700-1850,* Countryside Books, Newbury, 1991

Chapter 4. Fighting the French 1793-1815

Cordingly, David. *Billy Ruffian,* Bloomsbury, London, 2003

Fox, Sarah Prideaux. *Kingsbridge Estuary & Rambles in the Neighbourhood,* Kingsbridge, 1864

Kitchen, Frank. *The Napoleonic War Signal Stations,* Mariners' Mirror, Vol. LXXVI, pp337-344, 1990

Tracy, Nicholas. *The Naval Chronicle Vol. 1 1793-8,* Chatham Publishing, London, 1998

Chapter 5. The Preventive Service at East Prawle and Rickham

Fairweather, James. *Salcombe & Neighbourhood,* Salcombe, 1884

Luscombe, Ellen. *Myrtles and Alloes,* GP Friend, Kingsbridge 1861

Shore, Henry. *Smuggling Ways and Days,*1892, EP Publishing re-print 1972

Chapter 6. Farming & Fishing, Milling & Mining

Burte, Waite & Burnley. *Devon and Somerset Mines, Metalliferous and Associated Minerals 1845-1913,* Univ. of Exeter Press, 1984

Dickinson, M.G. *A Living from the Sea: Devon's Fishing Industry and its Fishermen,* Devon Books, Tiverton, 1987

Greenhill & Mannering. *The Chatham Directory of Inshore Craft,* Chatham Publishing, London, 1997

Fox, Harold. *The Evolution of the Fishing Village: Landscape and Society along the South Devon Coast 1086-1550,* Leopard's Head, Oxford, 2001

Hamilton Jenkin, A.K. *Mines of South Devon Vol. 1 Southern Area,* David & Charles, Newton Abbott, 1974

White, Walter. *A Londoner's Walk to the Land's End,* Chapman and Hall, London, 1855

Chapter 7. Saving Life at Sea in Victorian Times

Kingsbridge Gazette, Western Morning News. *Contemporary news reports*

Farr, Grahame. *Wreck and Rescue on the Coast of Devon,* D. Bradford Barton, Truro, 1968

Larn, Richard. *Shipwrecks of the Devon Coast,* Countryside Books, Newbury, 1996

McDonald, Kendall. *Shipwrecks of The South Hams*, Wreckwalker Books, Thurlestone, 2002

McDonald, Kendall. *Dive South Devon*, Underwater World Publications, Teddington, 1995

Mitchell, Peter. *The Wrecker's Guide to South West Devon Part Two,* Sound Diving Publications, Plymouth, 1992

Chapter 8. Mayhem & Bloodshed in East Prawle 1872

Kingsbridge Gazette, Western Morning News. *Contemporary news reports*

Chapter 9. Prawle Signal Stations 1868-1913

Bowen, Frank. *His Majesty's Coastguard*, Hutchinson, 1928

Board of Trade. *The 1931 International Code of Signals Vol. I For Visual Signalling,* HMSO, London, 1932

Lloyd's of London. *History of Lloyd's Signal Stations*, Manuscript no. 31670, Guildhall Library, City of London, no date

Chapter 10. The First World War

Kingsbridge Gazette. Western Morning News. *Contemporary news reports*

Bowen, Frank. *His Majesty's Coastguard*, op. cit.

Farr, Grahame. *Wreck and Rescue on the Coast of Devon*, op. cit.

London, Peter. *U-Boat Hunters, Cornwall's Air War 1916-10,* Dyllansow Truran, Truro, 1999

Wasley, Gerald. *Devon in the Great War 1914-18*, Devon Books, Tiverton, 2000

Chapter 11. Between the Wars

Kingsbridge Gazette, Western Morning News. *Contemporary news reports*

McDonald, Kendall. *Shipwrecks of The South Hams*, op. cit.

Mitchell, Peter. *The Wrecker's Guide to South West Devon,* op. cit.

Chapter 12. The Second World War

Pearce Peter. *Salcombe - War Window,* Harpocean 1989

Wasley, Gerald. *Devon at War 1939-45*, Devon Books, Tiverton, 1994

Chapter 13. Prawle Coastguard Station 1951-94

Kingsbridge Gazette, Western Morning News. *Contemporary news reports*

Chapter 14. Safeguarding the Coast Today Websites:

www.salcombelifeboat.co.uk/   www. nci-prawlepoint.org.uk
www.nci.org.uk   www.southdevonaonb.org.uk
www.nationaltrust.org.uk   www.southwestcoastpath.com

INDEX OF PLACES AND WRECKS

Page numbers in italics refer to illustrations.
All the place names and wreck sites are marked on Maps 1 to 3

Places

INDEX

Places *(continued)*

Wrecks